Princess Caraboo

Mary Wilcox of Witheridge, Devonshire, alias Caraboo.
Drawn and engraved by N. Branwhite.

Princess Caraboo

A Narrative of a Singular Imposition, Practised Upon the Benevolence of a Lady Residing in the Vicinity of the City of Bristol, by a Young Woman of the Name of Mary Willcocks, alias Baker, alias Bakerstendht, alias Caraboo, Princess of Javasu

Illustrated with two portraits, engraved from drawings by E. Bird, Esq. R.A. and Mr. Branwhite

John Matthew Gutch

Waking Lion Press

ISBN 978-1-4341-0324-6

The views expressed in this book are the responsibility of the author and do not necessarily represent the position of the publisher. The reader alone is responsible for the use of any ideas or information provided by this book.

Published by Waking Lion Press, an imprint of The Editorium

Waking Lion Press™, the Waking Lion Press logo, and The Editorium™ are trademarks of The Editorium, LLC

The Editorium, LLC
West Valley City, UT 84128-3917
wakinglionpress.com
wakinglion@editorium.com

Contents

QUI VULT DECIPI DECIPIATUR.[1]

The following Narrative, having been compiled in great part from conversation, it has in many instances been printed verbatim, as it was spoken or dictated by the party; many tautological, ungrammatical and vulgar expressions may therefore occur, for which the indulgence of the reader will no doubt be granted.

J.M.G.

---

1. "Let him who wishes to be deceived, be deceived."

The Amazing True Story of Princess Caraboo

On Thursday evening the 3rd of April 1817, the Overseer of the Poor of the parish of Almondsbury, in the county of Glocester, called at Knole Park, the residence of Samuel Worrall, Esq. to inform that Gentleman and his Lady, that a young Female had entered a cottage in the village, and had made signs, that it was her wish to sleep under its roof; but not speaking a language, which its inhabitants or the Overseer understood, the officer thought it right to refer to Mr. Worrall, a Magistrate for the county, for his advice; knowing also, that there was a man servant residing in Mr. Worrall's family, who was conversant with several foreign languages, and who could probably comprehend that in which the stranger spoke. The female was in consequence ordered to be brought up to Knole Mansion, but to which removal she shewed signs of strong reluctance; and when there, refused for some time to enter its doors. After some entreaty, she was prevailed upon to go in, and was presented to Mr. and Mrs. Worrall; who, with their servant, were unable to understand the language in which she addressed them; but intimated to her by signs, that they wished to ascertain, whether or not she had any papers in her possession; upon which she took from her pocket a few halfpence, with a bad sixpence, and implied, that she had nothing else. She had a small bundle on her arm containing a very few necessaries, and a piece of soap pinned up in a bit of linen. Her dress consisted of a black stuff gown with a muslin frill round the neck, a black cotton shawl on her head, and a red and black shawl round her

shoulders; both loosely and tastefully put on, in imitation of the
Asiatic costume; leather shoes and black worsted stockings. The
general impression from her person and manners was attractive
and prepossessing. Her head small; her eyes and hair black;
forehead low; nose short; complexion a brunette; her cheeks
faintly tinged with red; mouth rather wide; white teeth; lips
large and full, under lip a little projecting; and her chin small
and round. Her height about five feet two inches. Her hands
were clean, and apparently unaccustomed to labour. No ear-
rings, but the marks of having worn them. Her age appeared
about twenty-five. After a short consultation, Mr. and Mrs. W.
deemed it most advisable to send her for the night to a public
house in the village; and as Mrs. W. felt much interested by
her apparent distress, she ordered her own maid and footman
to accompany her, it being late in the evening, and to request
that the landlady would let her sleep in a private room, and
provide her with a good supper and a comfortable bed; and
that Mrs. W. would call upon her early the following morning.
The young woman seemed much fatigued, and walked with
difficulty. Upon being shewn into the parlour of the public
house, she was particularly struck with a print on the wall,
representing the Annana, and made those present understand,
it was a fruit of her own country, the representation of which
afforded her much pleasure.[1] Upon some preparation being
made for her supper, she expressed a wish that she preferred
tea; and before she partook of it, she covered her eyes with her
hand, and appeared to repeat a prayer, bowing her head at the
conclusion. Upon a second cup of tea being poured out, she refused taking it, until the cup was thoroughly washed; and when
she drank it, she repeated the same form of prayer with much
seeming devotion. When shewn to the room in which she was
to sleep, she appeared reluctant to go to bed, and pointed to the
floor; but upon the landlady's little girl getting into the bed, and
making her understand the comfort of it, she undressed, and

---

1. The Ananas (*Ananas sativus*) is the pineapple.

after kneeling, and appearing to say her prayers, she consented to lie on the bed. At seven the next morning Mrs. W. walked down to the public house, and found the stranger sitting by the fire, apparently very disconsolate, and as she thought with strong traces of sorrow and distress on her countenance, though she expressed much joy at the sight of Mrs. W. and accepted the visible marks of gratitude a change of linen, which Mrs. W. had brought for her. While her breakfast was preparing, the Clergyman of the parish, who had heard of her arrival, came in, bringing with him several books, thinking it probable she might recognize some one of the countries described in the plates they contained; and upon looking them over, she gave the spectators to understand, that she had some knowledge of the prints which were descriptive of China; but made signs, that it was not a boat, but a ship which had brought her to this country. Gaining very little information from this enquiry, Mrs. W. determined to take her back with her to Knole, and keep her under her roof, till something satisfactory transpired concerning her; and upon being invited, she followed Mrs. W. again exhibiting signs of reluctance and apprehension. Upon passing through the church-yard in her way to Knole, she tried, if the church door was open, and seemed much disappointed to find it fastened. Upon her arrival at Knole, she was led to the housekeeper's room, where the servants were at breakfast; and observing some cross-buns on the table (it being Good Friday) she took one, and after looking earnestly at it she cut off the cross, and placed it in her bosom. Upon Mrs. W.'s return from church, she summoned the young woman before her; and fearful of imposition, she attempted to interest the stranger by addressing her in the following soothing and compassionate language; "My good young woman, I very much fear that you are imposing upon me, and that you understand and can answer me in my own language; if so, and distress has driven you to this expedient, make a friend of me; I am a female as yourself, and can feel for you, and will give you money and clothes, and will put you on your journey, without disclosing your conduct to any one; but it must be on condition that you speak the truth. If you deceive me, I think it right to inform you, that Mr. W. is a Magistrate, and has the power of sending you to prison, committing you to hard labour, and passing you as a vagrant to your own parish."—During this address, the countenance of the stranger evinced an ignorance of Mrs. W.'s intentions, at the same time, making it apparent that she did not comprehend what Mrs. W. had said to her; and she immediately addressed Mrs. W. in her unknown tongue.—Mrs. W. then attempted to ascertain her name, by writing her own upon paper, and placing it before her, and pronouncing it several times, and putting a pen in her hand, intimated her wish, that she would write her name; but this she declined, shaking her head, and crying CARABOO, CARABOO, pointing to herself. Upon shewing her some of the rooms at Knole, she appeared delighted at seeing some pieces of furniture with Chinese figures, &c. upon them, making signs that they belonged to her country, or that she had been in the country from whence they came. At dinner she declined all animal food, and took nothing to drink but water, shewing much disgust at meat, beer, cyder, &c. On the following day (Saturday) it was thought advisable to take her into Bristol to examine her before the Mayor at the Council House; where no discovery could be made of her country or language, or whence she came, or whither she was going.[1] She was therefore in the regular mode

---

1. During her examination there was an observation of a magistrate present, which impressed her very forcibly, and which probably first induced her to persevere in acting the character she had assumed. The magistrate declared, that her language and manners were such as he had never before heard or seen.

It is not inappropriate to the developement of the imposture here also to mention, that it appears on her first essay to have been her intention to personate a French character. Before she had left the confines of the city, passing through Park Row, she encountered two or three of the French lace-makers from Normandy, who have established a manufactory in that part of the city. She watched their movements, and perceived that every body stared at them. This was food enough for the impostor's inventive genius. She fixed her eyes on the French

of commitment of persons in such situations, taken to Saint Peter's Hospital, the receptacle for vagrants and the poor of the city of Bristol. Here she remained till the following Monday, and it is well authenticated, that during her continuance in this house, she refused food of every description. On the Monday Mrs. W. whose solicitude for the welfare of her strange and singular guest had rather increased than diminished, went to Bristol and visited her at the Hospital. Her friendless situation had in the interim become public, and several gentlemen had called upon her, bringing with them foreigners of their acquaintance in the hope of discovering who she was. One gentleman who had travelled much in the East, and was about to embark immediately from Bristol to Malta, was trying to converse with her, when Mrs. W. called at the Hospital. This gentleman, some weeks after he left Bristol, addressed a letter to Mrs. W. on the subject, and the impression which this interview had made upon his mind was so strong, and is by himself depicted in such lively colours, that the insertion of his letter entire, in this place, will best explain what passed on this occasion.

"MADAM, "*Leith,* 16th *June* 1817.

"The peculiar case of the unknown female foreigner, who at present is fortunate enough to enjoy the shelter and protection of your hospitable roof, must naturally excite in the breast of every feeling creature emotions of interest and of sympathy. These emotions I perhaps feel in a double degree, from having seen her when in distress. I never can forget the circumstances of my first interview with her, nor

---

girls' peculiar head-dress, and it immediately occurred to her, that in the garb of a *foreigner* she might obtain that which was denied to an English-woman. She soon twisted her handkerchief into a turban, *outlandished* her general attire, and set off on the Glocestershire road. After walking a few miles, a gentleman accosted her; and perceiving that she was fatigued, took her to the next public-house, and gave her meat and spirits and water, which he, not being as yet an *Hindoo,* demolished *a la Françoise,* for she was now a French woman!

the gratitude she so eloquently expressed on recognizing you, Madam, in the Hospital at Bristol.

"Probably, Madam, you may have no recollection of me, and were it not that I have been an eye-witness of your goodness, I should hesitate much to use the liberty which I now do in addressing you on this subject. You must, however, be so kind as pardon me for my intrusion, and believe that I should not have troubled you, had I not felt extremely interested in the fate of your protegée.

"I left England a few days after I had the pleasure of seeing you in Bristol, and on my return to this country, about a week ago, I found, in an Edinburgh newspaper, a full account of all the circumstances attending this unknown lady, since she was found near the Knole. This revived, or rather added to, my desire of finding out her country, and I think, at least, that I have got a clue to it.

"I think her *name* is not *Caraboo*, as stated in the newspapers, but rather that that is her *country*. I consider that she comes from the Bay of *Karabouh*, on the eastern coast of the Caspian Sea, and situated in Independent Tartary. She may easily have come from thence by the Persian Gulf, or still more easily by the Black Sea. The latter I consider by the far more likely, as many vessels (many hundreds) have come from the Black Sea to the European ports in the Mediterranean, since the commencement of the present year. I leave these observations, Madam, to your consideration. She might be able to recognize the place I have mentioned on a map, or she might know the names of those places in the immediate vicinity. But you are better able than I am to decide on the manner, that this ought to be gone about. I therefore beg to remit it to yourself, and trust that some good may arise from the hint I have taken the liberty of giving to you.

"I request again, Madam, that you will pardon my presumption in addressing you; and if you will have the goodness to do so, might I still further presume to beg of you to let me know, by some means or other, any thing that you may think proper respecting this interesting fair one.

"I am, with the greatest respect,

"Madam,

"Your most obedient humble Servant,

"J.S."

At the Hospital, it is but justice to remark, that the most humane attentions, which are allowed of by the house, were shewn to the stranger. Finding she rejected the usual food, eggs and other delicacies were provided for her. But she was firm in her refusal of all kinds of nourishment; and she neither eat or drank, or slept on the beds of the Hospital, while she remained there. Mrs. W. still feeling a lively interest in her fate, determined upon again removing her, and had her taken to the office of Mr. W. in Bristol, where she remained during ten days, under the care of Mrs. W.'s housekeeper. Daily efforts were made to discover her language and country, but without effect. At last a foreigner of the name of MANUEL EYNESSO, a Portuguese, from the Malay country, who happened to be in Bristol, was introduced to her, and he declared that he could undertake to interpret her language. The tale, this impostor pretended to extract from her, was, briefly, that she was a person of consequence in her own country, had been decoyed from an island in the East Indies, and brought to England against her consent, and deserted. That the language she spoke was not a pure dialect, but a mixture of languages used on the coast of Sumatra, and other islands in the East. This Manuel Eynesso in short invented a story so plausible, and one so well suited to the imposition the girl had determined to practice, that Mrs. W. was induced a second time to take her to Knole, intending to communicate the particulars of her history, as far as she could collect them, to some respectable individual at the East India House, and extend her protection to her till the truth of her story could be developed. She accordingly resumed her old apartment at Knole. And from the 3rd of

April till the 6th of June, she not only ingeniously and most effectively contrived to deceive her benevolent hostess, her family, and their domestics; but she had the address to delude and highly interest numbers of visitants at Knole, who were eager and solicitous to examine and listen to the unknown foreigner. There was no one who took a greater interest in her fate and adventures, than one gentleman who had made several voyages to the East-Indies, who was conversant with every creek and harbour in those seas, and well acquainted with the customs of China. This gentleman committed to writing the following particulars, either extracted from the girl at various times by signs and gestures; or as it now appears, in the warmth of his anxiety to discover her history, he most probably assisted her in the creation and composition of them.

That her name was CARABOO; that she was the daughter of a person of rank, of Chinese origin, by a Maudin, *alias,* a Malay woman, who was killed in a war between the Boogoos (*Cannibals*) and the Maudins (*Malays.*) That whilst walking in her garden at Javasu, attended by three sammens (*women*) she was seized by the people of a pirate prow, commanded by a man of the name of Chee-min, and bound hand and foot, her mouth also covered, and that thus she was carried off. That her father swam after her; and in pursuit shot an arrow, which killed one of her women, who were taken on board with her. That she wounded herself two of Chee-min's men, with her crease, when she was seized; one of whom died, but the other was recovered by the Justee (*a Surgeon.*) After eleven days she was sold to the captain of a brig called Tappa Boo; the brig sailing during the transaction; she being conveyed from one ship to the other in a boat. That after four weeks the brig anchored at a port,[1] remained there two days, and having taken on board four female passengers sailed again, and in five weeks more anchored at another port,[2] where the four females were landed;

---

1. Supposed to be Batavia.
2. Supposed to be the Cape of Good Hope.

that they staid three days, and then sailed for Europe, which she reached in eleven weeks; being near some part of the coast of England, in consequence of the ill usage she experienced, she formed and carried into execution the resolution to jump overboard, and she swam to shore. That the dress she had on consisted of a gown worked with gold; a shawl on her head of the same description, which was exchanged by an English woman, the door of whose house was green; for which she gave her a black stuff gown, a cotton shawl, and several other articles; in which dress, after wandering about for six weeks, during which period she was frequently admitted into various houses, she found her way to Almondsbury.—Her father's country she called Congee (*China*)—her own island, from whence she was taken, she called Javasu, and that of her mother the Maudins (*Malay.*) She described her mother's teeth as being blackened,[1] her face and arms painted, and that she wore a jewel at her nose, with a gold chain from it to the left temple; which decorations her mother wished to have adopted for her, but her father would not consent. That he had three more wives, and that he was carried on the shoulders of Macratoos (*common men*) in a kind of sedan or palaquin, and wore a gold button in his cap, with three peacock's feathers on the right side of his head, a gold twisted chain round his neck, to which was suspended a large square locket of amber-coloured stone, set in gold. That she herself wore seven peacock's feathers on the right side of her head. Upon giving her some calico, she made herself a dress in the style she had been accustomed to wear.[2] It was very short in the petticoat, the sleeves uncommonly wide and long enough to reach the ground, but only half-scored up, and confined at the wrists. A very broad band round the waist, which she described as embroidered, as was the bottom of the petticoat; embroidery also was round the bosom, and round the open part of the sleeves. She wore no stockings, but open

---

1. From chewing betel nut.
2. *Vide* Mr. Bird's representation of her.

sandals on the feet with wooden soles. She pronounced her father's name *Jessu Mandu,* and her own *Sissu Mandu,* which was afterwards changed to *Caraboo,* in consequence of her father having conquered his enemies. That he had the command of soldiers, and that when any people approached him, they made their salam or obeisance on both knees, lifting the right hand to the right temple, and that they presented fruit in a dish balanced upon the points of their fingers, kneeling upon both knees to her father, and upon one to herself. That servants salam to a gentleman with the right hand to the head, to ladies with the left. That during her father's dinner the Macratoos played to him upon an instrument of music, consisting of a reed, through which they blew, and which was affixed to a kind of harp held between the knees and played upon with the fingers. That her father's complexion was white; he was 47 years old [1] ; her mother's Malay colour, very yellow or brown. That the Boogoos (*Cannibals*) were black. That when they took white prisoners, they cut off their heads and arms, and roasted them by a fire, round which they danced, and then eat them. When shewn the drawing of an idol, the object of worship at Prince's Island, she expressed the greatest abhorrence, and implied, that she did not do so; but that she worshipped ALLAH TALLAH; and that her mother told her, if she did as her father did, who prayed to an image, that she would be burnt in the fire. She described the Pirate Prow as having only one mast and no guns; her colours Venetian war. Cheemin, the commander, was copper-coloured, wore a turban, short petticoat trousers, and a kind of scarf thrown over his shoulders. That Tappa Boo's was a dark complexion; he had long black whiskers, and long black hair plaited down the back, and knotted at the end in a bow; that he wore a kind of seal-skin cap, and an ear-ring in his right ear. That his brig had guns, but did not know how many; there were about 40 men, among whom was a Justee (*a Surgeon;*) the vessel carried Spanish colours. The ladies, who were passengers

---

1. This she explained by tying knots upon a string.

used to talk and write, but she could not understand them, neither did they understand her. That she was very ill after Tappa Boo bought her, for which she was cupped in the back of her neck, and bled in the arm and wrist; her hair also, which was extremely long, was cut off, and she was confined to her bed a considerable time. That her illness was occasioned by her crying and great unhappiness in consequence of her miserable and forlorn situation. She explained, that at the same time when Tappa Boo bought her of Cheemin, that he bought a bag of gold dust; and that the water was so shoal or shallow at Javasu, that a large vessel could not come near. She described the sails of Cheemin's boat as seamed up and down, and of a different shape from those of Javasu, which were of matting or rush; that the Chinese were made across with split Bamboo sticks. Upon having a plate of the flags of all nations shewn to her, she fixed upon the Venetian war as Cheemin's; the Spanish as Tappa Boo's, and the Chinese as her father's.

When made sensible, that she was requested to point out the colours hoisted at the different ports at which she stopped, she placed her fingers upon her closed eyes, and shook her head, as much as to say, she never saw them, making it understood at the same time, that she was kept below in the ship. She expressed much pleasure at the sight of a Chinese chain purse, which was shewn to her, which she instantly recognised, and described as belonging to her father's country; also a rose-coloured scarf, which she put on, first in the Chinese and afterwards in the Javasu fashion; in both instances veiling her face. She sometimes twisted her hair and rolled it up on the top of her head, fastening it with a skewer. She also acknowledged the pierced ivory fans, and the Chinese puzzle, Indian ink, sattin stone, garnets, white and brown sugar candy, and green tea, as belonging to her father's country; and that cinnamon or cassia, white pepper, rice, mother of pearl, flying fish, and an apple differing from ours, as belonging to Javasu; and that the cocoa nut, long pepper and coral,[1] were of her mother's or the Malay country.

---

1. The different articles here specified, with many others, were all

CARABOO PRINCESS OF JAVASU,

She described the dead as not being buried in coffins at Javasu, but that they were placed in the ground; and when made to

---

placed before her; and with very few exceptions, she described the countries, from which they came, or in which they were in use.

understand, that if she was to bardoo (*die*) here, she would be buried flat in a box, as she had seen a corpse in the church-yard, she expressed much dislike and apprehension. She marked time by knots on a string in a peculiar manner, and by this means pointed out the periods and distances of her voyage. A chart of the supposed places she stopped at, as drawn by herself, is inserted in the appendix.[1] She pourtrayed the method of writing in her own country by a sort of reed upon the back or leaf of a tree; and that in Congee they wrote with a Camel's hair pencil and Indian ink. A vocabulary of words and the meanings to which she applied them, collected from her own mouth during the period of her visit at Almondsbury, and after her detection, is inserted also in the appendix. She was always consistent and correct in using them in the same sense, meaning or object. Her Autograph of Mary Baker is also subjoined.

Such was the detail of the Princess's life, previous to her supposed arrival in England. But there were of course many singular occurrences, which happened during her residence at Knole, and which tended in no trifling degree to confirm the description, which she had given of herself, as well as the manners and customs of the country from which she represented herself as coming. A few of the most prominent and curious were the following:

The Gibberish language, in which she made herself understood, was aided in a very striking manner by gestures and animation of countenance, which it is impossible to describe; and singular to relate, that during the ten weeks which she resided at Knole and in Bristol, she was never heard to pronounce a word or syllable which resembled her native tongue. Mrs. W.'s housekeeper, who slept with her, never heard at any interval any other language or tone of voice than that which

---

1. She afterwards acknowledged, that she drew this chart by a gentleman leading her from one place to the other, and prompting her as it were to the delineation.

she first assumed.[1] The servants once said in her hearing, that they would lie awake, to listen if she talked in her sleep; and on that night, and afterwards, she feigned to be asleep, and began talking her gibberish. In returning from Bristol sometimes in Mrs. W.'s carriage, she was so fatigued, that she fell asleep; but Mrs. W. though she awoke her suddenly, never found a word or a sound escape her, which could lead to detection. In the choice of her food she was also equally consistent and uniform, and affected much peculiarity and nicety.—

She dressed every thing herself; preferred rice to bread; eat no meat, drank only water and tea. She was very fond of Indian curry, which she frequently dressed herself, and made very savoury. She refused a pidgeon (*a Rampue*) that was dressed, but having a live one put into her hands, she cut off its head, which she buried together with its blood under the earth, and then dressed and eat the other part. Fish she served in the same way. She always said her prayers night and morning, and rigidly fasted every Tuesday; on which day she contrived to ascend to the roof of the mansion at Knole; frequently at the imminent peril of her life. Ablutions she was particularly fond of: she was once seen to plunge into a pond in Knole Park, and she regularly knelt down and washed her hands and face by the side of it. She was equally correct and clean in washing the utensils in which she eat and drank. The tenants, and farmers, and their daughters about Knole and at Almondsbury grew very fond of her, and she often visited them with Mrs. W.'s leave, but they never found her tripping or off her guard, either in her conversation or general manners, always observing the custom of washing her tea cup, &c. One day she appeared to be highly exhilirated, and gave the servants to understand, that it was her

---

1. One of Mrs. W.'s sons, who suspected her to be an impostor, and who one day declared before her, that she was a cheat, provoked her to exclaim, "*Caraboo, no cheat;*" but this did not occur, till after she had so long resided in Mrs. W.'s house, as to enable her to imitate the sound of several English words and phrases, and of course led its inmates to believe that she must have learnt them there.

father's birth-day, and that he was forty-seven years old. During her stay she used to exercise herself with a bow and arrows, and made a stick answer to a sword on her right side, the bow and arrows slung on her left shoulder. She oftentimes carried a gong on her back, which she sounded in a very singular manner, and a tambourine in her hand, the sword by her side and a bow and arrow slung as usual, her head dressed with flowers and feathers, and thus she made it appear she was prepared for war. During her residence at Knole, she heard people say, that this was the custom abroad, and so she imitated it. Sometimes she would row in the boat in the pond at Knole, using the oars very dexterously.[1] She learned her salams, or mode of greeting from what she overheard; and from the observations of people, who had been in the East, and who conversed with her, she appears to have modified her system of deception. One gentleman happening to observe, that if she was an Hindoo, she would make her salam with an inclination of the head and both hands gradually brought down from the forehead; and if a Malay, she would put her hands on the side of her head, she immediately put her hand on the right side to a gentleman, and on the left to a lady. When dancing she would assume an infinite variety of attitudes, far from destitute of elegance; bend her body in numberless shapes, but never offensive to delicacy or propriety, occasionally dropping on one knee, and then rising with uncommon agility, holding up one foot in a sling, and performing a species of waltz with the most singular twists and contortions. She presented a plate of fruit, holding it on the points of her fingers and thumb with peculiar grace. Mrs. W. was one evening absent from Knole on the day of a wake in the parish, and on her return found her missing. The gardens were searched, and she was discovered sitting in a high tree, in which she explained herself to have climbed, because all the

---

1. After the discovery of her cheat she declared, she often wished to have prevailed on Mr. W.'s Greek servant to get into the boat with her; she thought he always suspected her, and she meant to have given him a ducking.

females in the house had gone into the village, and she feared contamination from the men. In the garden also she one day constructed an arbour as a temporary place of worship, which she sprinkled with water and threw her shawl over her head when she knelt to prayers. She never omitted a grace at any of her meals. Mr. P. of Cathay, in the city of Bristol, a gentleman who had visited Malay several years since, was supposed to be able to throw some light on the business. He brought with him to Knole a Malay crease (or dagger) which Caraboo with great animation recognised as belonging to her country; and her desire to have it in her own possession was extreme, but from prudence it was denied her; this denial seemed only to increase her desire. She placed the dagger to her right side (where the Malays wear it) which confirmed to this gentleman, that she perfectly understood the custom, though not the language of that country. In fencing she was particularly expert. Mr. W., who esteemed himself a tolerable fencer when young, could seldom disarm her when using the long sword. At times she exercised herself with a sword in the right hand and a dagger in the left. Among other occurrences which shew the dexterity with which she seized, and acted on what she heard, is the following; a gentleman observed, that it was customary in the East to stain the points of a dagger with vegetable poison; the next time a dagger was put into her hands, she went to a flower stand, and rubbing a couple of leaves between her fingers; applied the juice to the point, and then touching her arm, pretended to swoon!—She, in truth, conducted herself so correctly, and her manners were so fascinating, that she soon became caressed, and perfectly domesticated at Knole. She waited on Mrs. W. at her toilette, and indeed had the whole range of the house; books of different descriptions, brought or procured for the purpose of ascertaining who she was, were constantly left in her way, and from these she read, and, no doubt, copied the characters which she wrote. The grand lever, however, by which she performed all her deceptions, was, her own NATIVE ENGLISH, which she could and did distinctly HEAR and profit by, tho' she never spoke it. Another singular key to deception was, her astonishing command of countenance and self-possession. A jocose clerical gentleman, of Bath, tried to move her by FLATTERY: he drew his chair close to her; looked steadily and smilingly in her face, and observed "You are the most beautiful creature I ever beheld. You are an angel."—Not a muscle of her face moved; no blush suffused her cheek; her countenance was motionless.— After three weeks residence at Knole, she was one morning missing. The *cacoethes errandi* had returned upon her; and she was panting for the shores of America. She had accordingly decamped; but returning again in the evening with a bundle of clothes, and her shoes and hands dirty, she gave Mrs. W. and her servants to understand, that she had dug them up from a place where she (*risum teneatis amici?*) had buried them, to hide them from the Macratoos!—The truth was, that during her short absence, she had hastened to Bristol; but fearing she might be pursued from Mrs. W.'s, she cut across the country, by the Duchess of Beaufort's Woods, at Stoke, making her way through hedges, and over ditches, till she reached her old landlady's house in Lewin's Mead, Bristol.—From thence, packing up a trunk, which she had left in her care, she ran to the Quay to look for a ship, the captain of which she had been in treaty with for her passage to America, before she set out on her vagrant expedition to Almondsbury;—but the vessel had sailed! Returning to her lodgings, she paid her arrears of rent; had her trunk conveyed into Thomas-Street; sent it to her father by one of the Exeter waggons, and returned with her bundle of clothes to Knole, with all possible expedition. Was it a wonder the girl should have been foot sore and sick?[1] Having disposed

---

1. Why did not Mrs. W. on her return try to trace her out, by advertising a description of the clothes which she brought with her, is here a natural question? Indeed, in the course of the Narrative, several occurrences are stated, which, had they been noticed at the time, must have led to detection. This Mrs. W. does not disavow; but there were other personages deceived as well as Mrs. W. who had not her motives of humanity to plead in excuse, and to whom the motto in the title page equally applies—"*Qui vult decipi decipiatur.*"

of her heavy baggage she had nothing to look to but herself and bundle, and was thus ready for a march at a moment's notice, whenever circumstances occurred which were likely to lead to detection. Soon after her return she was taken very ill, and the attendance of a respectable medical gentleman of Bristol was necessary. This gentleman had also been in the East, but during the painful hours of sickness, she contrived to elude even his scrutinizing endeavours to discover her country and language. During her illness, in the presence of Mrs. W. and two medical men who came to visit her, one suspicious circumstance arose: it suddenly occurred to one of them to try the effect of alarming her, by stating to Mrs. W. her extreme danger, and that it was probable she could not survive twenty-four hours longer; when in an instant her face became crimsoned. This circumstance, however, lost much of its weight from the maid, who constantly attended her, stating, that such flushings had taken place five or six times every day during the continuance of her illness; an occurrence very common in typhus fever. After her recovery the sympathy of Mrs. W.'s Greek servant was much excited in behalf of Caraboo. He had previously supposed her an impostor, and had constantly behaved towards her with coldness and suspicion. His unbelief, however, began now to waver; and as if to recompense her for his former unkindness, he treated her with double attention, pity and respect.

Disappointed in her intended escape to America,[1] she appears to have reconciled herself to stay a little longer under Mrs. W.'s protection. But whether she grew tired of the confinement at Knole; whether she dreaded discovery from the frequent visits she paid to Bristol, in company with Mrs. W. when she might chance to meet the eye of her old landlady, of Lewin's Mead; or whether she heard under Mrs. W.'s own roof of an intention of sending her to London, to be examined at the East-India House;

---

1. What an impression her visit would have made, had the Princess of Javasu escaped to America or elsewhere, leaving the imposture undiscovered?

or under whatever apprehensions she may have laboured, she began to meditate another escape. And on Saturday the 6th of June, she again took her flight. Mrs. W. undoubtedly felt much uneasiness at her disappearance. She had as before taken with her not a pin or a ribbon, which did not belong to her. Indeed her principles of honesty have been found unimpeachable, in whatever situation of life she had been discovered. It was towards Bath, that she had now bent her way; and on the following Sunday Mrs. W. received information of the place to which her protegée had flown. She again determined to reclaim her; and Mrs. W. reached Bath on Sunday afternoon. Here she found the Princess at the very pinnacle of her glory and ambition, in the drawing-room of a lady of *haut ton*.— Cervantes himself could not have expected the realization of so fine a scene. What was the situation of Sancho Panza at the Palace of the Duchess, in comparison with the Princess of Javasu in the drawing-room of Mrs. ——? Oh! that we had the pen of a Foote or a Garrick to portray the inimitable acting and the consummate deception of this day's adventure. The drawing room was crowded with fashionable visitants, all eager to be introduced to the interesting Princess. There was one fair female kneeling before her, another taking her by the hand, another begging a kiss!—The girl afterwards declared, that this was the most trying scene she ever encountered, and that on this occasion she had more difficulty to refrain from laughing, and escape detection, than in all the singular occurrences of her life. The same gentleman, who took down the detail of her pretended adventures before her arrival in England, saw her in the public-house in Bath, previous to her making her appearance in Mrs. ——'s drawing-room. Upon first noticing him, her spirits forsook her, and she burst into a flood of tears, which fell most copiously for some time, during which she kept her face covered with her handkerchief (from an apprehension no doubt that the discovery had taken place); so soon, however, as she was satisfied, that her enquirers were still in the dark, she recovered herself, and again proceeded as actively as ever in the imposition. "Can it be possible," says this gentleman, writing to Mrs. W. "that she should be deranged in her mind, and yet have been enabled to carry on her deception so long and with such consistency? We have heard of the power of maniacs to concert deep-laid plans with the greatest subtlety, but I recollect no one being carried on so successfully, for so long a time, and under such a variety of circumstances."

Dr. Wilkinson of Bath, was another of the *Cognoscenti,* who was led likewise by the same love of the marvellous, which had duped so many other of the visitants at Knole, to try his skill at developing the character and nation of the unknown foreigner. And the publicity which the Doctor gave to his visit by detailing in the public prints a description of her person, manners, and situation was eventually the means of leading to a detection of the imposture. The learned Doctor was no less fascinated, than the gentleman from China, with the character he had beheld. The two letters, which he published, form so excellent a corollary to the farce that was acting, that it would be inexcusable in this place to omit them. They were as follow:—

"TO THE EDITOR OF THE BATH CHRONICLE.
SIR,
The present inexplicable appearance of a young female foreigner in the vicinity of Bristol, having excited considerable curiosity; as I have had the opportunity of being in her company, and of obtaining what information is at present known, from her benevolent protectress, Mrs. W. of Knole, at whose house she resides; I am desired to request, you will be so obliging as to insert these particulars in your Chronicle, with the hope that they will be copied into many provincial papers; so that by such a general dissemination, they may be read by some who have observed a female, corresponding to the description here given; and may ultimately lead to the developement of those circumstances, which have placed a most interesting female in a situation truly distressing.
I am, Sir,

Yours,
C.H. WILKINSON.
June 1st,
Burlington-street, Bath.

"About two months since, a female presented herself at
the door of a cottage at Almondsbury, near Bristol: the door
being open and a couch in view, she made signs of a wish
to repose herself. She appeared in a very debilitated and
distressed condition, as if exhausted by much fatigue. The
cottagers, not comprehending her language, reported the
case to Mrs. W. who resides about a mile from Almondsbury; and that lady kindly visited, and gave orders for the
most humane attention to be paid to her. Her language was
equally unknown to Mrs. W. but her appearance and graceful manners so interested that lady, that she took her under
her own roof, where she has since experienced the most
unremitting kindness. Her head is small; her eyes and hair
are black; her eye-brows finely arched; the forehead low;
nose rather short; complexion very trifling sallow, rather
more corresponding to a brunette, with a pleasing colour
on the cheeks; a sweet smile; her mouth rather large; her
teeth beautifully white and regular; her lips a little prominent and full, under lip rather projecting; her chin small
and round; no ear-rings, but marks of having worn them;
her hands unaccustomed to labour; in height five feet two
inches.—Her dress consisted of a black stuff gown, with
a muslin frill round the neck; a black cotton shawl on the
head, and one red and black round the shoulders; leather
shoes and black worsted stockings. She appears to be about
25 years of age; her manners are extremely graceful, her
countenance surprisingly fascinating. Such is the general
effect on all who behold her, that, if before suspected as an
impostor, the sight of her removes all doubt. Her mode of
diet seems to be Hindoostanie, as she lives principally on
vegetables, and is very partial to curry; she will occasionally

take fish, but no other animal food; water is her beverage; and she expresses great disgust at the appearance of wine, spirits, or of any intoxicating liquors: whatever she eats, she prepares herself. She is extremely neat in her attire; is very cautious in her conduct with respect to gentlemen; never allows them to take hold of her hand, and even if their clothes should casually come into contact with hers, she retires from them: when she takes leave of a gentleman, it is by the application of the right hand to the right side of the forehead, and, in like manner, on taking leave of a lady, it is with the left hand. She appears to be devout; and on a certain day in the week is anxious to go to the top of the house, and there to pay adoration to the sun from the rising to the setting. She casually saw a dagger; and, as if anxious to inform her kind patroness of all the customs of her country, which she calls *Javasu,* she placed the dagger to her right side. She fences with great dexterity, holding the sword in her right hand and the dagger in her left. She is very fond of bathing; and swims and dives with considerable activity. She carries about with her a cord, on which some knots are made, like the Chinese *abacus,* which afterwards gave rise to the sliding beads, the *suon puon.* She writes with great facility from left to right, as we are accustomed. She has made Mrs. W. understand, that in her country neither pens or paper are used; but what is supposed to be a camel hair pencil and a species of papyrus. Soon after her residence at Mrs. W.'s house, she was attacked with a typhus fever, and was placed under the care of Mr. Mortimer, an eminent surgeon of Bristol: upon her recovery, pleased as she must have been at his kind and constant attention to her, she wrote him a letter of thanks, calling him, as a doctor, *Justee,* and herself *Caraboo.* All the assistance to be derived from a Polyglott Bible, Fry's Pantographia, or Dr. Hager's Elementary characters of the Chinese, do not enable us to ascertain either the nature of her language, or the country to which she belongs: one or

two characters bear some resemblance to the Chinese, particularly the Chinese *cho,* a reed: there are more characters
which have some similitude to the Greek, particularly the
ι, π, and ε; different publications have been shewn to her,
in Greek, Malay, Chinese, Shanscrit, Arabic, and Persic, but
with all she appears entirely unacquainted. Her letter has
been shewn to every person in Bristol and Bath versed in
oriental literature, but without success: a copy was sent to
the India-House, and submitted by the chairman of that
Company to the examination of Mr. Raffles, one of the best
oriental scholars, yet he could not decypher it: the original
letter was sent to Oxford, and the members of that Univer-
sity[1] denied its being the character of any language; it has
been by some conjectured as being an imperfect Javanese;
others have supposed it the style of the Malay of Sumatra.
From my own observation, although entirely unacquainted
with any single character of her writing, I have deemed
her more resembling a *Circassian;*[2] her countenance, her
complexion and her manners, favour such a supposition;
and probably her appearance here may be connected with
the Corsairs who have been hovering about our coast. She
has by signs intimated, that she was on board a ship, and
so ill-treated, that when she came within sight of land, she
jumped over-board and swam ashore. She also, in the same
manner, expressed, that she was ill on board, her hair cut
off, and an operation on her back performed: I examined
the part, it had been scarified, but not according to the
English mode of cupping, or to any European manner with
which I am acquainted; the incisions are extremely regular,

---

1. Every gentleman who perused it very properly, and without a
moment's hesitation, pronounced it a Humbug.

2. Dr. Wilkinson was not singular in this opinion, if this will be
any consolation to him; as the following letter will testify. This letter
was one among twenty, all addressed to Mrs. W. expressive of equal
anxiety and interest in the fate of the stranger.

and apparently employed with the caustic, a mode of cupping adopted in the East. The Supreme Being she stiles *Alla Tallah*. All who have seen her are highly interested about her. A fac-simile of her letter is placed in the Kingston Pump-Room for examination. I beg leave to observe, that I have seen her write, and she writes with grace and facility.

"P.S. Since writing the above, I have been informed of the following circumstances:—*Caraboo* quitted Mrs. W.'s house for one whole day, to procure a few clothes, which she signified to Mrs. W. that she had buried, to conceal them from the *Macratoos* (rogues); the distance must have been considerable, as her feet were blistered; and the violent illness which followed, was owing to the fatigue. Mrs. W. whose opportunities of observation have necessarily been superior to those of any other person, is persuaded her father is Chinese, and that her mother, who is dead, was Malay; that her father's name is *Jesse Mandue,* and that he is a man of considerable consequence in his own country.— *Caraboo* describes a gold chain he wears about his neck."

"*Edinburgh,* June 14th, 1817.
"MRS. WORRALL, MADAM,
"I wish to be excused for making so bold as to trouble you with a letter, making a few inquiries respecting the female foreigner, whom, being destitute, you have so kindly, humanely and generously sheltered under your hospitable roof. I have carefully read the description given of her in various Scottish publications, and the supposition that she is a Circassian (as I myself was brought up in that country) makes me particularly anxious to know about her. Her features, food, mode of eating; the caution in her conduct with respect to gentlemen; the use she makes of her hands in taking leave of ladies and gentlemen; her disgust at wine, spirits, and intoxicating liquors, all favour Mr. Wilkinson's opinions. Her mode of worship too, on the house top with

her face towards the east, resembles that of the Circassians, were it not that she pays adoration to the sun. The
Circassians worship and pay adoration to none other, but
the true God, facing Mecca; under the impression that, on
their Prophet Mahomet's account, the Author of all things
on earth makes that spot his chief abode; the God they
worship, they call ALLA-TALLAH. It is probable the female
foreigner, in this respect, may be misunderstood; instead of
worshipping the sun, she, like them (the Circassians) may,
with her face towards Mecca, worship the same God, as it
evidently appears from her giving her God the same name,
ALLA-TALLAH, by interpretation, GOD ALMIGHTY. If thus
misunderstood, her mode of worship likewise supports the
idea, that she is a Circassian.

"There are, however, other things which make her being
a Circassian doubtful. Her dress, as far as I can understand
from the newspapers, differs. I do not recollect ever seeing
a Circassian female wear a black stuff gown, with a muslin
frill round her neck, inclined at all to a continental fashion.
The worsted stockings also, to the best of my knowledge,
are no part of a Circassian dress; but these articles have
not been made sufficiently plain, and a description of the
clothes she afterwards brought, has been wholly omitted.
The next most doubtful of all is her writing. All the while
I was in Circassia, I neither saw nor heard of more than
two of their women being capable of writing, and even
those wrote with an Arabic character from right to left;
but she, the female foreigner, is said to write from left to
right, with a character as yet unknown, and that with great
facility. I am unacquainted with either of the names Javasu,
Malay, Jesse-Mandue and Caraboo, as applied; though
some of their parts may have meaning, either in Tartar
or in Circassian. The part Java, of the name Javasu, in
Circassian, may either signify a surface of any thing, or the
second person imperative mode of the verb to drink; the
latter part, su, signifies water in Tartar. The part Mal, of

the name Malay, signifies a sheep in Circassian; the other, ay, is an interjection in Tartar and in Circassian, of the same meaning as in English. The first part, Jesse, in the name Jesse-Mandue, in Tartar signifies an owner; to the last part I can give no signification. The first part of the female foreigner's name, Cara, is either a Tartar adjective signifying black, or the second person imperative mood of the Tartar verb to look; the last part, boo, signifying this or that, is a pronoun in the same language. It will not be improper here to observe, that by the name alone, it is impossible to know a Circassian; names being given at random, made up with words of two or three languages, and often none at all. Having stated the reasons for my thinking her a Circassian, and those which make me doubtful, I shall now, in Roman Characters, set down a few questions in the Circassian and Tartar languages, which being carefully read to her, by the observation of the rules given, may lead to a discovery whether she be a Circassian or Tartar.—Rule for the Circassian questions: sound all the letters as in English; the vowel a, as in fat; u, as in full; and g, hard before e and I. Along with the questions I shall set down the translation.

"CIRCASSIAN.—1st. Adigivzar uptshera? Do you understand Circassian—2d. Uadiga? Are you a Circassian.—3d. Set etsh ukyka? What land do you come from.—4th. Ui yader adigit? Was your father a Circassian.—5th. Etsar Setit? What was his name.—6th. Ui yaner adigit? Was your mother a Circassian.—7th. Ui tshema etsar set? What is the name of your country.—8th. Adigivzer uptshama, ege unjessa pesselthahema juap kuzat? If you understand the Circassian language, give an answer to the words now spoken. Note. Sound u, in the last word, as in urn.

"Rule for the TARTAR questions: sound a again as in fat; the dipthong oi, as in oil; e marked thus ē, as in me; e marked thus ĕ, as in Eden; g hard before e, as formerly.— 1st. Nogoi tillen bēllasĕnma? Do you understand the Tartar language.—2d. Nogi sĕnma? Are you a Tartar.—3d. Nĕ jerden shukhansen? From what land are you.—4th. Atang negoi ĕdĕma? Was your father a Tartar.—5th. Ata nĕ ĕdĕ- What was his name.—6th. Anang nogoi pĕshy ĕdĕma? Was your mother a Tartar woman.—7th. Sĕnung jĕrungnung ata nēdēr? What is the name of your country.—8th. Egĕr nogoi tillda bēllzung, sorrahan? humba juab bĕr? If you understand the Tartar language, answer the questions asked you. Note—Sound the u, in shukhansen (3d q.) as in luck. I hope the above will afford some degree of satisfaction; but if she understand none of the sentences I have set down, her giving the Supreme Being the name Alla-Tallah will be a wonder to me, being a Circassian word, and one familiar to me.

"Have the goodness to send me an answer to this letter, with a description of all her clothes, some of the characters she writes, a few words of the language she speaks, and, if a Circassian, her answers to the question I have given.

"Thus you will oblige your humble Servant,

"A.B."

The following is a copy of the Doctor's second letter:

"Last Saturday evening, about seven o'clock, *Caraboo* arrived at the Pack-Horse Inn, in this city. It appeared, that the driver of a caravan invited her to ride; and at about three miles distance from Bristol, on the road to Bath, she got into the vehicle, but would not admit of any assistance from the driver. When brought to the above Inn, considerable embarrassment was experienced from the inability of comprehending her language: but the landlady paid the kindest attention to her, and at length comprehended her wish, *from her delineating a tree, which was fortunately conjectured to be the tea tree.* The arrival of a stranger under these circumstances soon excited considerable attention, and particularly that of a gentleman, a Mr. Carpenter; who, having a few minutes before read an account given in our last Chronicle, supposed this person to be the one described, and in consequence sent information of her to Dr. Wilkinson. The Doctor received it too late to visit her that evening; but between seven and eight o'clock the next morning, he went to the Inn, and found her at breakfast with the landlady; she immediately recognised him, and Dr. W. adopted those measures which would the most expeditiously intimate to her kind patroness, Mrs. W., the situation of *Caraboo*. As soon as breakfast was finished, she disappeared: Dr. Wilkinson casually met her alone in the Circus; she walked about for some time, and then returned to the Inn; where she readily followed Dr. W. into the dining-room, and he left her in charge of a female in the house. About twelve o'clock, it appearing that public curiosity would be considerably excited, and that probably *Caraboo* would be annoyed by many visitors, two ladies, who had been sitting by her for sometime, and who experienced for an interesting female, thrown, by circumstances yet unknown, on a country where the inhabitants and the language are equally strange to her, those feelings, which shew in the most inestimable point of view the human mind, offered the protection of their house in Russell-street, and thither *Caraboo* was immediately re-moved in a chair. Her confidence, by the kind treatment she received, was soon excited; her countenance became animated with smiles of gratitude; and she endeavoured *to explain to the ladies the customs of her country, by actions the most graceful, and by manners highly fascinating!* In the evening, her benevolent protectress appeared: immediately on the sight of her, the situation of *Caraboo*,—the graceful manner in which she prostrated herself to solicit pardon for having left Mrs. W.'s house,—most sensibly affected every person present. Upon inquiry, it appears, that *Caraboo*, anx-iously wishing to return home to her father, her husband, and her child, thought this could sooner be accomplished by her removal to some other place. All the circumstances

attending her leaving Knole evinced a mind formed on the most correct principles of honour; various little articles and trinkets, which had been presented to her, also money in a purse, were all left in the greatest order in her room; and she quitted Knole without a single farthing in her pocket.— Upon every occasion she has shewn a great dignity of mind; and her astonishing power of interesting all around her appeared most satisfactorily, in the great interest excited in the truly amiable mind of her protectress. When *Caraboo's* absence was ascertained, Mrs. W.'s anxiety was indescribable; ten or twelve persons were sent in different directions to find her; and as soon as the intimation arrived of her being in Bath, the carriage was immediately directed to the same place.—Every circumstance, which has transpired since our last communication, additionally contributes to the proof, that *Caraboo* is the character, she represents herself to be; and those who have paid the greatest attention to her have no doubt, but that she is a native of one of the Japanese Islands, called Javasu, and that her father is Chinese! From some circumstances it would appear, that her mother was of European descent, probably Portuguese; she is evidently acquainted with the principles of Christianity; she described the crucifixion and resurrection.—What has been reported of a similar female having been seen at Cork, upon inquiry turns out incorrect; *nothing has yet transpired to authorise the slightest suspicion of Caraboo, nor has such been ever entertained, except by those whose souls feel not the spirit of benevolence, and wish to convert into ridicule that amiable disposition in others!* It ought to be remarked, that, from the indefatigable attention of Capt. Palmer, and from the journal of Mrs. W. a more correct account of this surprisingly interesting female may be expected."
    "Bath, June 9, 1817."

The *Bath Herald,* after noticing the arrival of the impostor in that city, says,—"It was now thought advisible to adopt some effective measure for the relief of this *most interesting creature;* an appeal to the East-India Directors was determined on—Dr. Wilkinson proceeded to London on the charitable mission on Tuesday—and was to be followed the next day by Caraboo herself." At the very moment that the Doctor's letter was printing at Bath, CARABOO was making a full confession of her imposture at Bristol!—What a rebuke for a Philosopher!

The unexpected arrival of Mrs. W. in the drawing-room in Russell-Street, Bath, was another occurrence which severely put to the test the girl's ingenuity and self-command. Mrs. W. burst suddenly into the room, and in an instant Caraboo recognised her benefactress. She fell on her knees with that graceful prostration which she so well and so frequently practised, and embraced Mrs. W. with an ardour of attachment and an appearance of joy and gratitude, which captivated every spectator. She seemed to have forgotten the brilliancy of the scene around her, and as if overpowered by the ingratitude she had shewn in leaving Mrs. W.'s roof, she rushed through the company, and in an instant disappeared. She was followed down stairs by Mrs. W., and when she found herself alone with her in the parlour below, she had the address again to reconcile Mrs. W. to her escape, by making her believe it was her anxiety alone to re-visit her parents at Javasu, which induced her to run away. Mrs. W. left Bath with Caraboo in her company the same night; and the relation to Mrs. W. of the girl's exploits in the drawing-room, the commendations of such a host of spectators, aided by her apparently contrite expressions of sorrow, served to rivet stronger than ever the regard of Mrs. W. and to convince her, that her protogée was indeed an unfortunate Princess of Javasu. Far different must have been the conflict of feelings passing at this time in the bosom of Caraboo herself. Proud of, and conscious, that on this occasion her powers of deception had surpassed all former exertions, she was at the same time equally conscious, that as her fame was extending, the hour could not be far off, when the developement of such a scene of duplicity must arrive. She had heard at Knole, that the newspapers contained a description of her person and conduct, and an invitation to the public to interest themselves in her behalf; she felt, that suspicion might be awakened as well as sympathy. Her tears at Bath were the first symptoms of alarm and compunction which she betrayed; and on the Monday morning, after her return to Knole, Mrs. W. observed her, not without some degree of surprise and apprehension, turn the lock of the chamber-door, after she entered Mrs. W.'s dressing-room. Her heart misgave her at this moment; and Mrs. W. has not now a doubt upon her mind, but that at this period the girl meditated an acknowledgment of the duplicity of her conduct. The occurrence nevertheless pass'd by, without any remark from Mrs. W. and Caraboo resumed her usual cheerfulness throughout the day. The bubble, however, was on the eve of bursting.

The re-publication in the *Bristol Journal* of Dr. Wilkinson's first letter, led to the detection. Mrs. Neale, with whom Caraboo had been lodging, read in that newspaper, with no little surprise and amusement, the freaks of Caraboo; and in an instant recognised the character of her *quondam* lodger. On Monday morning she called upon Mr. Mortimer, and informed that gentleman of her suspicions, and produced such irrefragable proofs of her knowledge of Caraboo, that Mr. M. the same evening, thought it prudent to communicate the intelligence to Mrs. W.; and singular to relate before Mr. M. left the parlour at Knole, a youth arrived from Westbury, the son of a wheelwright there, who had met with the girl on her first expedition to Knole, and who well remembered, that when in his company spirits and water were not quite so repugnant to her taste, as they had been at Knole. This double disclosure flashed immediate conviction on Mrs. W.'s mind, and coupling these occurrences with the agitation of Caraboo in the morning, Mrs. W. did not now hesitate to probe such suspicions to the bottom. She accordingly determined to wear the same appearance of friendship and kindness towards Caraboo during the evening, and in the morning to take her to Bristol and confront her with Mrs. Neale. Under the idea that she was going to Mr. Bird's to finish the sitting for her

portrait, which that gentleman was painting, she accompanied
Mrs. W. to that city, and they alighted at the appointed time at
Mr. Mortimer's, instead of Mr. Bird's. The discovery was speedy
and decisive. Mrs. W. having conversed with Mrs. Neale and
her daughters went alone into a room with Caraboo, told her
of the damning proofs she had now obtained of her being an
impostor, and after having tried once more in her gibberish to
interest Mrs. W. by saying "Caraboo, Toddy, Moddy (*father* and
mother) Irish," she found she could not succeed; and Mrs. W.
being about to order Mrs. Neale up stairs, she acknowledged
the cheat; begging that Mrs. W. would not cast her off, or suffer
her father to be sent for. This Mrs. W. promised upon certain
conditions; one of which was, that she would instantly give
a faithful detail of her former course of life, disclose her real
name, her parentage and history. Mrs. Neale being dismissed,
the girl immediately commenced a narrative to Mr. Mortimer,
in which, to account for her knowledge of Eastern customs, she
attempted to shew, that she had resided four months at Bombay,
and also at the Isle of France, as nurse in an European family.
But Mr. Mortimer having visited Bombay, soon detected her, and
she refused at that time to communicate any further particulars.
To another gentleman, however, she soon was prevailed upon
to enter into a second detail; of which the following narrative
contains the leading circumstances:

That her name was MARY BAKER; that she was born at
Witheridge, in Devonshire, in 1791, and received no education,
being of a wild disposition. At eight years of age, she was
employed in spinning-wool; in the summer months, she often
drove the farmer's horses, weeded their corn, &c. From her ear-
liest years she had always an ambition to excel her companions,
whether at any particular game, playing at cricket, swimming
in the water, or fishing, &c. At the age of sixteen, her father and
mother procured her a situation at a farm-house (Mr. Moon's,
Bradford, near Witheridge). She staid there two years, looking
after children; at this place, she often carried a sack of corn or
apples on her back, endeavouring to do more than the labouring

men. She left that place because she had only ten-pence a week; she offered to stay for a shilling. After which she returned to her father's house. Her father and mother used her ill on account of leaving her place; and accordingly she left them and went to Exeter, where she knew no one. Being a stranger there, she inquired for a place, having a written character with her from her late mistress, and was directed by a fish-woman, whom she met in the street, to Mr. Brooke's place, a shoemaker, in Fore-street. Being a country girl, Mrs. B. liked her appearance very much, but was afraid that she was an apprentice that had run away from her mistress. She offered to give her 8. a year, if she returned to her father's house for a fortnight, that she might inquire whether she was an apprentice or not; and at the expiration of it, she hired her. As she was expected to wash, iron, and cook, to which she was not accustomed, she only staid there two months. Being at this time very fond of finery, she applied the wages which she received in the purchase of clothes, and then returned to her father's. On her return he was much hurt to see her in white, and her mother insisted on her taking it off, which she would not do. She staid there only six days, during which time she saw her friend, and her old master and mistress; but being dressed in white, they said, that she had dishonestly procured it. Knowing her innocence, and not enduring to hear this, she again decamped and returned to Exeter. From whence she wandered through different parts of the country, not knowing whither to go. She had left her clothes at her father's, and had no money in her pocket, and went begging at the different houses: some gave her a little money; some said, that it was a pity for such a young creature to wander about the country; others proposed taking her up as a vagabond and horse-whipping her, at which she cried very much, and was almost resolved to destroy herself. With this determination she strayed from the highway down a lane, and took her apron-strings and tied them together, and fastened them to a tree to tie round her neck. She either heard, or fancied that she heard, "Cursed are they that do murder, and sin against the Lord." She then untied the string, and proceeded on her journey. Being very uneasy and unhappy, she was heard crying a great deal, and at length met with an elderly gentleman; he said, "My pretty girl, what is the matter with you, crying so? Where are you going?" She told him her story, and the late particulars of her being about to hang herself. He was much agitated, and reasoned with her strongly about the wickedness of it, and gave her five shillings, saying, "Go away in peace: put your trust in the Lord, and he will never forsake you." With that money she went into lodgings, and rested herself three days at Taunton.—All this was between Exeter and Taunton; but being very young, she did not recollect the names of the places.

From Taunton she proceeded on her journey to Bristol, and pursued her plan of begging from house to house.—When she got money, she slept in lodgings; otherwise in a hay-loft, and often between hay-ricks. Thus she arrived in Bristol; where, having nothing to eat, and being very hungry, she was directed to the Strangers' Friend Society, at a Mr. Freeman's, by the Drawbridge. (She always took care to conceal her own and her father's name.) Mr. Freeman asked her various questions and the reason of her leaving her home, which she did not tell him. He gave her four shillings to get lodgings that night, and desired her to come in the morning, that he might inquire about her friends. Instead of going to him, she left Bristol, as she did not chuse to be discovered to her relations. Thence she travelled on the London road, and nothing particular occurred before her arrival at Calne; where she unfortunately begged at a constable's house, who took her up to return her to her friends. He intended to take her to the justice in the morning, to swear her to her parish; but, when he went out for something in a yard behind the house, she made her escape through the window. She thus proceeded within thirty miles of London, when she was taken very ill, being over-fatigued, and having had bad food. Being unable to continue her journey, she sat down by a hedge, until a waggoner passing by with two women in a waggon, who said, that he had seven children of his own, and did not know to what they might come, so he let her ride to London in the waggon. They offered her something to eat and drink, but being ill she was unable to take any thing. When they arrived at Hyde-Park Corner, she and the other people left the waggon, as the waggoner dared not suffer them to ride into London. The women were unwilling to leave her, but asked her where she was going. On her saying, that she knew no one, and knew not where to go, they each took her by the arm and led her to a house, until it was dark; and when it was dark, took her to the door of St. Giles's Hospital. She sat down on the step, and they left her. She remained there about one quarter of an hour, when the watchmen came. They asked her who she was, and took her to the watch-house; but she could not reply, through illness and fatigue. They then brought Mr. Burgess, a physician of the hospital: he shook his head and said, that she was in a very dangerous state, and ordered her to the hospital; where she remained many months insensible in a brain fever. The doctors shaved her head and blistered it; and the nurses told her, that during her insensibility, they inquired of them every morning whether she was not dead. After getting better, she asked Mr. Burgess to let her go down stairs in the yard for a little air. He said, that she was not strong enough; but as she persisted, he told her, if she would carry a tea-kettle that was on the fire to the end of the ward, he would let her go down. The doctor did not know that there was hot water in it. She fell down, and scalded herself. The doctor caught her, as she was falling. After which she kept her bed a whole month, and when she got better, she was removed from the fever to the decline ward., where she remained till she had strength to go out. When it was time for her to leave the hospital, the matron and nurse asked where she was going, and whom she knew; and they spoke to the clergyman[1] who attended the hospital, and he recommended her to some ladies, who got her a place at Mrs. Matthews's,

---

1. This will afterwards be discovered to have been the Rev. Mr. Pattenden.

No. 1, Clapham Road-Place. There she remained three years. Her father and mother not hearing from her all this time, the clergyman who took her out of the hospital, having asked about her friends, sent down a letter to know, whether it was true. To which an answer was returned, that her father was living and her mother very ill, through fretting about her. The gentleman continued the correspondence with her friends. Mrs. Matthews being a very good mistress taught her to read, gave her religious tracts, and permitted her to use the books in her bookcase. Her daughter Betsy wrote letters for her to copy, when she came home from school, which she learnt very fast, and spent her leisure time in reading, and made no acquaintance with any one.—A Jew lived next door, and at length she got intimate with his cook, and they continually were talking over the garden wall in the absence of their mistresses. She never went out during these three years, except once in three months, when she was allowed to see the clergyman and lady, who got her the place. They always called her their adopted child; and she was as such introduced to any one that was there, when she called upon them. At the conclusion of the three years, there was to be a Jew's wedding at the Horns, at Kennington, and this cook asked her to go; which she resolved to do, be the consequence what it would. She asked her mistress, for the first time, for leave, which she refused; saying, that being young and inexperienced she insisted on her not going. She felt hurt at the denial, and began to contrive means of going. Mrs. Baynes, a shop-keeper, was very intimate with the gentleman and lady that called her their daughter: she had lately lain in. She went out and got a woman to write her a note, desiring her to write, that Mrs. Baynes would be obliged to her mistress to let her go to the christening, which was on that day. She put it in the post, and it was received the next morning. She carried it to her mistress, and obtained leave to go. She told her to be at home at eight at night. She dressed herself and went to the Jew's wedding, which her mistress did not suspect, and returned at the time appointed. She said nothing that night, but the next morning

asked the child's name, which she said was Edward Francis.—
Mrs. M. asked whether there was a large party; she said yes;
on which she coloured, which excited suspicion. She went to
inquire, and detected the whole procedure. On her return, she
desired Mr. Pattenden to call. She was very angry, and scolded
very much. On which, fearing to see Mr. P. she left the house
without her bonnet and waited about, thinking that he would
be gone in half an hour, but he stopped all night. All which time
she was in the back lane. From thence in the morning, as she
was walking up and down, Mrs. M. saw her and sending for her,
told her, that staying out that night was an additional offence.
She then took her clothes, and left her. She went to a widow
woman, who made feathers and straw-bonnets, and supplied
her mistress, where she staid eight days. This woman wrote to
her father for her, informing him that she had left her place,
and sent him for her clothes; saying, that she wanted nothing,
and had left England with a travelling family.—She had often
observed the Magdalen, in Blackfriars' Road, and conceiving
it to be a nunnery, was resolved to get into it. She asked this
woman about it, and she said that women went there the first
Wednesday in a month. She called and knocked at the door
on the appointed day, where there were many young women
besides. As they entered the room, their bonnets & caps were
taken off. They asked her, how long she had gone on in that
way? How long she had been on the town?—the meaning of
which she did not comprehend—she said she was sorry for her
faults. They talked very seriously with her, and made her cry.
They told her, as she was so young, if she was truly penitent,
they would take her in, which her tears prevented her from
answering. Then one of them said, poor thing, she is very much
affected, we will admit her. On her admission she received a
bit of paper with *admitted* written on it, and then was ordered
to deliver it in the next room. She was taken into a bath, and
every thing was taken from her, and the Magdalen dress put
on her; which was a stuff gown, a white tippet, and a plain
bordered cap, plaited round the face. She was there six months,

and acted as a sort of housemaid. Soon after, one of the women was talking with her about her former life; on which she said, is it possible? She replied, you are as bad as we are, otherwise you would not be in this house. Endeavouring, therefore, to vindicate herself, they acquainted Mr. Prince, who was the minister. He interrogated her; she replied, that she suddenly left her place, and came to the Magdalen. He accused her of falsehood. She told him the particulars, and she was summoned to the board the next day, and was then expelled the house. The Bishop confirmed her when there, and she learned most of the Magdalen hymns. They then delivered her clothes, and a pound note which she had in her pocket, when she went in. She thought of going into the country to her father and mother, in room of getting a place; but instead of going directly there, being afraid of walking over Hounslow Heath, on account of robberies and murders, then prevalent, she changed her own clothes at a pawn-broker's for men's, and equipped herself in them. To try whether her sex would be detected, she went to a house to ask if there was a place vacant for a young man, in which she succeeded, and was laughed at as a little man. They told her of a person that did. She was introduced into the parlour, where there were three gentlemen and four ladies. Her hair being short, she powdered it and combed it in front; and took the ear-rings out of her ears. They asked her age, and how she was so short a man. They said, they liked her, but they would not take her into the house, because she looked so very wicked. Leaving this, she tried her success by begging as a man, and thus she started, till she got to Salisbury Plain, where she met two men on horseback, who asked her, whether she had any money? She replied no, and was going to ask them to give her some. They asked whether she would go with them, and enter into their service, viz.: to look after their horses, when they came home, and go out with them, when they went out by night. She asked where they went to. They said, that if they found her faithful, they would open the secret to her; but as they did not know that she was a woman, she accepted the

offer, determined to find out their business. When they came
home to a small house in a forest, they gave her something
to eat and to drink; and when she had been there about half
an hour, four more came in. They asked, whether she could
fire a pistol? She told them no, that she had never learnt to
fire. They gave her a pistol, bidding her to fire it off, showing
her how to do it; at which she was frightened. They called her
a chicken-heart; and said, that she would not be fit for their
service, unless she plucked up a bold heart and courage. She
fired off the pistol more dead than alive, and screamed out that
she was murdered.—They threatened to destroy her, having
ascertained thereby her sex, if she did not tell, whether she
did not come there as a spy: then she fell on her knees, told
them every thing, and begged pardon; hoping that they would
let her go free. On which the captain drew a sword and said,
if she would swear by the sword, and all the powers above
never to betray them, they would let her go free. Which she did.
They gave her a guinea and five shillings, and she went off. She
arrived at Exeter, without any thing fresh. Thence she went to
Witheridge, in woman's clothes, to see her father and mother.
They were much surprised to see her, conceiving she was with
the travelling family. She said, that she left them, and lost her
luggage by the coach. On which her father gave her back her
clothes. They wanted her to get a place in the country, to which
she agreed; and she and her mother went to Crediton, and got
a place with Mr. Pring, a tanner. She lived there three months;
but left it on being obliged to do things out of her place, viz.
being obliged to heave the hides in the yard out of the cart. She
then went to Latford, and then she heard of a place two miles
off, at a little village named Spring (near Calne).—There she
hired herself, and staid three months.—In that severe winter
with the deep snow, when, for many weeks, they could not get
to the butcher's or to market, they sent her one night to see if
she could go, as they had killed most of their poultry, &c. She
went as far as she could, and sunk in the snow. Not being able
to get up, she staid there all night, and expected never to be

found. In the morning she was extricated, taken home, and put to bed. On which she resolved to leave the country; gave them warning, and went back to Exeter. There she inquired for service. She was at Attorney Sandford's, Goldsmiths' Street, as a cook: here she stopped also three months, and went away because the fire did not agree with her, and set off for London. She went into lodgings and tried to get a place. She succeeded at one Mrs. Hillier's, fishmonger, Dark-house Lane, Billingsgate. One day she went to the stationer's to get some books, where she saw a gentlemanly-looking man. He asked every particular about her, when she was gone, her name, &c.: which the people of the shop told him. In the evening, she received a letter from him, and he called frequently to see her, when her mistress was absent, and often met her. She left her place suddenly; and after two months acquaintance got married.[1] They were married by a Romish priest. They took lodgings, and stopped about a month in London. From whence they went to Kingston, where they had lodgings; and from thence they travelled all round to Brighton, &c. &c. From there to Battledore (*supposed* Battle) a few miles from Brighton. He then gave her some money to take her to London; her husband proceeding to Dover, and from thence to Calais, promising to write and send for her, which he never did. She then went to London, and returned to service, at Mrs. Clark's, the Crab-tree, in Tottenham-Court Road, where she remained till she was taken in labour. Mrs. Clark got a coach, and took her to the City-Road Hospital. She was there three weeks, and returned to Mrs. Clark's, with the child, who advised her to take lodgings and get the child into

---

1. Whether she was really married to this foreigner, or whether he seduced, and afterwards deserted her, has not been clearly ascertained. There is little doubt, but that it was from this man who had probably associated with Malays, or was acquainted with their language, that she picked up the Eastern words and idioms which she used, as well as that knowledge of some Asiatic customs, which so effectually enabled her to effect her imposition. This person's name was Bakerstendht or Beckerstein.

the Foundling. She went to the Foundling, told them, that she was unable to support the child, and knew not where the father was gone. She went three Wednesdays following, and the child was admitted on the last. They gave her a guinea, and, after waiting a month, they gave the child Foundling clothes, and she left the child there. She again went to service, at Miss Ferret and Miss Field's, in Thornhaugh-Street, near Russell-Square.— Every Monday, between ten and four, she went to inquire for the health of the child. The child shortly died, and then she left London. She took a coach and returned to Witheridge. She stayed there a week and three days, and her mother and self went to Exeter. Her mother carried her clothes for her to go to another place. She sent her box to Bristol, by the waggon, to be left till called for. She left Exeter and went towards Plymouth. She had not proceeded far, before she saw some gypsies on the road. Having had nothing to eat, she asked for something, and took some tea with them. She stopped three days with them; during which time, they endeavoured to persuade her to continue with them, assuring her, that she would make her fortune. They endeavoured to persuade her to do many things with them, which she rejected, and accordingly left them.— Instead of going to Plymouth, after leaving them, she went across the country to Teignmouth; and from Teignmouth she went to Honiton, acting all the way the part of a foreigner, and begging thus at farm-houses. She avoided gentlemen's houses, lest she should be detected; and always wore her bonnet. In this disguise, she proceeded to Bristol. She had ten shillings with her, and being tired got on the stage-coach, six miles the other side of the city. She tried every where for lodgings, and was not suited for a long time. She met a woman, whom she asked for such, who took her to Charlotte Bennet's, near Lewin's Mead, who kept lodgings. She could not accommodate her, but a woman, who used to lodge there, was there at the time, and said, that she might sleep with her, in Lewin's Mead. Her name was Eleanor—,[1] she used to go out to work. She gave one shilling a week, and was there nearly three weeks. Then she did not pretend to be a foreigner, until one day, when, for a frolic, she dressed herself in her turban, and went out in the streets: she was with her; and they went begging, and she had five shillings given her, where she spoke her lingo. This was the only house in Bristol to which she went. Two or three days before, she went to the Quay, to inquire if any vessel was bound for America, and was answered, that there would shortly be two or three. One Captain said, he would take her for 5. to find herself, and there were many passengers going. He said, that the vessel would sail in fifteen days. Not having money to pay for her passage, she thought, that she would, under the garb of a foreigner, try to get money during those fifteen days to go there. She left her box at Mrs. Joseph's, and left Bristol, on Tuesday, and went towards Lamplighters' Hall, by Lord De Clifford's.—The people at Lord De C.'s wanted to take her in, but she would not, and went farther to a farm-house, where she dined with the farmer and his wife, on roast veal, greens and potatoes. After dinner, he sent his own daughter with her to Lord De Clifford's, to see if the French cook could understand her. She was loath to go in; the servants intreated her, but she would not: they offered something to drink, &c. The cook could not understand her; and happening to ask her if she was an Espagnol, and she answering *Si,* he said, she was a Spanish woman. One servant was going to take her to some Spanish families in Bristol, when she ran to get her bonnet, and made her escape through the fields, and slept in a labourer's house.[2] She overheard the labourer saying to his wife, perhaps she is a rogue, or a disguised man, or some one come to murder us; and she could not sleep all night for laughing. She thought, she should have died with laughing before the morning, as the

---

1. This was Eleanor Joseph, she had forgotten the real name of the person.
2. Mr. Yates's cottage, in the Lanes by the Cherry Orchards.

woman was nearly in fits, through fear that she was a disguised robber. In the morning, having had one cup of tea, she crossed the Marsh, and went on the Passage road. She met a man, who said, it was a fine morning: she answered him in her lingo. She had all this time her bonnet, not her turban. When they came to the village, he said, what a pity it was for her to go on without knowing any one, or being understood. By signs, they wanted her to go to a French governess, at a gentleman's house[1] just by, who concluded she was Spanish. She proceeded on her journey towards the Passage, until seeing a public-house, with a bench before it, as it was very hot weather, she sat herself down to rest. The mistress, by signs, begged her to come in, and refresh herself, which she did. The same man, who took her to the French governess, overtook her here. Some offered her one thing, some another; but she took nothing. The man, that ran after her, said, that she was a Spaniard, and that she must be fond of brandy, as much was distilled in Spain. They brought her a decanter of brandy. On making signs, no, they brought decanters of gin and rum, to see whether she liked either of them. She took a little rum and filled it up with cold water, and eat some biscuits. She proceeded on her journey to the Passage, the man accompanying her.[2] They met a soldier and another man, whom her companion asked, if he could speak Spanish; the man said yes, for he had been in Spain many years; and wished he were there now; he spoke to her; she answered him in her own language, and he replied, that she did talk Spanish, and came from Madrid Hill!!! He told the man, that she said, she had a father and mother, who were behind on the road; and seeing her touch a cow on the horn, he told her not to touch them, because they were not like those in Spain; he said, women rode cows in Spain. She proceeded till within three miles of the Passage, where finding herself so near to Wales, she

---

1. Mr. Llewellyn's.
2. This was the wheelwright's son who afterwards called on Mrs. W. to tell her, that in his company she had drank spirits.

wished to return back. She then took a paper from her pocket, that had been given to her the preceding day, with CHARLES HARVEY. Esq. Queen Square, French Consul, written; and made signs, that there she wished to go; but her companion declared, that he would see her safe one way or another, for he was paid by the French Governess to do so. They called at the same public houses, and had some beef steaks for dinner; after which she returned to the village, from which she had before started, and they gave her some tea; in came the French Governess, and another lady and gentleman, who though he had been in Spain could not talk Spanish; but from what the man narrated of the soldier, he believed her a Spaniard. He gave the man a direction to a Spaniard in Clifton, to take her there; she was obliged to accompany him to Bristol, where she was resolved to make her escape, and so made signs that she would go to the French Consul, whom the young man could not find. On his stopping to enquire of some acquaintance in Queen Square, she slipt round the corner, and hid herself behind one of the barrels on the Quay, till the man was out of sight. She then enquired in English for lodgings for that night, and the next morning she started for Almondsbury. About half ways, she took off her bonnet and put on her handkerchief as a turban: most people called her French. At a public house[1] where she stopp'd, they gave her beer. When she got on Almondsbury Hill, she went to a shoemaker's shop for lodgings, but they did not understand her, and put bread and butter and water before her. Then they shewed her to Mr. Hill's; they sent her away from thence to the Rev. Mr. Hunt's, who was not at home: she went in, saw a bed, and made signs that she wanted to sleep there; but Mrs. Hunt was alarmed at her appearance. They sent her to the Overseer, who offered her sixpence. She made signs she wanted not money, but lodgings. The Overseer sent her to Mrs. Worrall's: she objected to go there, fearful of being found out. The man servant was continually asked what language she talked. She went in at their invitation, and sat down in the kitchen.

---

1. Patchway.

[Her reception at Mrs. Worrall's, at Knole, has before been given.]

In her narrative to Mr. Mortimer, as well in that which has now been related, having asserted that her parish was Witheridge in Devonshire, and that the name of her parents was WILCOX; Mrs. W. before she proceeded farther in rendering any assistance, determined to ascertain how much of truth, and what there was fiction in the account she had given of herself, requested a respectable tradesman of Bristol to visit her parents in Devonshire; and from the minutes which this gentleman made on that occasion, the following particulars are extracted:—

On his arrival at Tiverton, where he had heard that the Rev. Mr. Dickens, the vicar of Witheridge resided, he introduced himself to him, and described the object of his visit. Mr. Dickens knew the parties well, and expressed much surprise that a girl, so uneducated as he knew Mary Willcocks to be, could so well have supported a part of such duplicity. Her father, he said, had always borne a good character, was an honest hardworking man, and her mother a sober industrious woman, who had brought up a large family; they were very poor; the father's trade a cobler, he had known them for the 25 years, he had been vicar of Witheridge. He had read in the Exeter paper the account of the stranger's arrival at Bristol, and little suspected that one of his parishioners could be the girl, who had excited so much curiosity. Mrs. Dickens offered to accompany the Gentleman to Witheridge, where they went; and on their arrival at the vicarge-house, Willcocks and his wife were sent for. Before the gentleman, acquainted them with the object of his visit & enquiry, they informed him, that they had four children—the eldest a son about 32, a daughter Mary 25, and another son and daughter 15 and 9 years old.—On asking if he could see their daughter Mary, they looked confused; and after hesitating, the father said, he could not fetch her, for she had left them, and he did not know where she then was. It was about eight years since she first left him, and he had seen her several times since, but could not tell the reason of her leaving him, the last time she went away. It was not on account of his beating her with a strap, though he had once done so, for going with another girl to a fair at Exeter. He had flogged her well about two years ago, for going there contrary to his consent. That, at the age of fifteen, she went into service with a Mr. Moon, of Exeter, where she remained upwards of two years, and then ran away to London. He heard of her going to London from a girl who ran away with her, and grew tired of her journey and returned; that he learnt afterwards, that his daughter was taken ill on her journey, that a waggoner gave her a lift to London, and set her down at an Hospital, where she was a long time confined in a frenzy fever; that the day on which she was to be discharged, a gentleman, whose name was Pattenden, was visiting a poor woman in the same ward; being informed of her forlorn and friendless situation, he enquired of her particulars of her life, and promised to ascertain the truth of them from Mr. Moon, and if she was correct, he would endeavour to place her in a respectable situation. He prevailed on the guardians of the house to let her remain there, till he heard from Mr. Moon. Mr. M.'s answer confirming her account of herself, and giving her a good character, he took her to his own home, and procured her a place very soon after, with a Mr. Matthews; Clapham-Road Place, where she continued three years. That her parents frequently heard from her; that she sent them a pound bill, said she was very happy and comfortable, and when she wrote, sent them money, whenever she could save a little before hand. They always heard she was very much liked, wherever she lived.

That on leaving Mrs. Matthews, she came down to Witheridge and staid a little while at home, and then went into service with Mr. Sandford, Attorney, at Exeter, with whom she lived sometime, and left him with a good character. She then went again to London, and Mr. Pattenden having promised always to befriend her, she applied to him, and he soon placed her in the service of Mrs. Field, where she staid a few months; again quitted London, and returned to her native place. This was about a fortnight before last Lady-day.

Upon the gentleman's asking, if her parents had ever the curiosity to make enquiries who Mr. Pattenden was, they said, yes; that a son of a neighbour, a linen-draper in London, had done so, and found him a highly respectable character, a Presbyterian Minister, much beloved in his neighbourhood. That when his daughter left them, she could not write, but Miss Matthews had taught her; that she learnt to read at a school in Witheridge; was always fond of her book, and when out of work spent most of her time in reading. When she returned to them from Mrs. Field's, they knew she had been married; she wrote them word so; that she had a child four months old, who died before she left London. Never saw her husband; told them, she had left him at Dover, and that she was come to take her leave of them, before she went to the Indies. Did not say whether she was going to the East or West-Indies. She gave them some money and took her leave, and they had never heard of her since.—Upon being asked if they observed any difference in her manners, or any thing particular in her conduct, during her last visit, the father said, she was very *learned,* and could talk French very fast: she used to talk for two or three hours in a morning to her sister in bed. He knew it was French, because the folks in the village said it was so. But he really thought, she was not always right in her head. Ever since she was fifteen years old, in consequence of a rheumatic fever, which affected her head, he believed she was not right in her mind. At spring and fall she was particularly uneasy, always wishing to go abroad. She was never fond of tippling, never drinking other but water. Upon asking for a sight of some letters which they had alluded to, the mother instantly fetched them, and gave them into the gentleman's custody. There is an allusion in one of them to a present, that her mother had sent her. Mrs. Willcocks did not remember what it alluded to, but the father brought to her recollection, that it was three fat ducks and a pint of cream, which they had sent to Mr. P.—who they thought had been her deliverer and saved her from ruin, by his kind attention and good advice.

The gentleman then explained to them the object of his visit, and the part their daughter had been acting.—They were much affected; were anxious to know if she had committed any other crime, and hoped the lady at whose house she was staying would forgive her, and endeavour to place her in some situation, where she might maintain herself; for which they should ever feel grateful, and hoped to hear of her future welfare, through the Rev. Mr. Dickens.

The following are the letters, which her parents placed in this gentleman's hands. The two first are written by herself; those which follow, are alike in the hand-writing, but have more the appearance of a male than a female character.

"My dear father and Mother and my Love and duty to my dear brothers and sister I hop i shall find you all in good helth. Ples give my Love to grandmother and ant burgess and all friends Im in most delightful place and my mistress Treats me with all Imaginable kindness and my youn miss is Larnd me to write and ihope ishall nax Letter isen belebl. To write befor I hve ver good friends but my dear Mother i m got so fat that you wel not lard now me but I wnt to now the situation that you Live in with it is beter now and it nas when i Live ther it was bad Enough then with I hop it is beter now and i hop you will send me letter to Let me now how all of you are but my dear father i hop hoo will kip my dear sister fom ple for it will be the raun of her for i never did my time pass mor agreeably for i do my work wil paleasure wen i hav dond reading for i never go yout yout is to church and i naver so happy when im bmy salf but my dear mother I whe you wer so happy as im I hop my dear brothers will never let you want for ant thin I wich it was in my por to mker you comfortable but my dear mother I have send you wan pond not and I hop it wall be acceptable presents wen my dear father I have got wan vever to beg of you that is to send my aged for i wich to now how hold im wich I her yous most humbly dutyf

Loving daugther Mary Willcocks Mr. Mathews clapham rod place kennington No 1 November 24

"Mrs. Baker would thank Mrs. Wilcock to call at Mr. Horsewell's Linen Draper No. 81 Fore-street Exeter to let her know if this arrive safe 22 Dec. 1811"[1]

"Thomas Willcocks

"Witheridge near Crediton Devon."

"Mary Willcocks

"Mr. Mathews Clapham road Place

"Kinnington N 1 August 19 1812

"My Dear Father and My Mother i hop you are wall as iam tho the blesed of god I have ben vary hill but Iam Much bater thenk The Lord for it Pleace to give My Duty and Love to My dear Brothers and sester and i hop they Are wall and i hop you will be so kind as to remember Me to ant Burgess and all Friends I want to Bed a favory of you if you pleace to sen me Word wre sally dinner live as I wich to see her I have very good friends so you see i hav got thee 3 Fathers ther is Mr. Pattenden you Mu Dear and i hope i have got a heavenly Father I hope you will tell me of any good that may Attend you give me opportunity to rejoice hide Not from me any evil that may befal you That i may mingle My tears with yours i Bend me down with gratitude for the Last Paternal gift you made me which has Proved My salvation and it will add Batterness to my Years force to my groans and sharpness to the stripe if the virtues and sufferings of this life are Not sufficient to atone for the last ast of disobedience May every happiness and comfort attend you My Last Prayers in this world will Be for those that have loved me wich I am your most obliged affestionate"

(No Signature.)

---

1. This sentence is in a different handwriting.

"London, July 1st, 1816.

"My dear Father and Mother,

"What apology to make I know not for my undutiful conduct, for which I beg your forgiveness. I have been travelling abroad with a family this long time back, and have lately returned from the Continent. You have, I believe, heard that I was married, and have got a young child about four months since, which we have called John Edward Francis. I am going to Norwich with my husband, who is a native of that place; but I am not sure whether we shall remain there or not, but I will write to you every three months, and let you know every particular of our situation. Give my love to my brother Thomas, and sister Susan: let me know what trade you intend to bind him to. I send you—as a small mark of my love and duty, and I shall send you in future, please God, half-a-crown a week; but it will answer as well to send it quarterly.

"I beg you will write to me directly, for fear I should happen to leave London before I receive your answer.

"I conclude with my love to brothers and sister, and kind compliments to all friends.

"Your ever dutiful daughter,

"MARY WILCOCKS."

"P.S. Direct for me to Mr. Paddington, No. 29, Coppice Row, Clerkenwell, London.

"My husband (Baker) whose christian name is the same as the child, sends his love and duty to you."

"London, Jan. 18th, 1817.

"Dear Sir,

"Being a friend and acquaintance of your daughter's, Mrs. Baker, who went to France before Christmas to her husband, she left me a pound note in charge for you, which I now enclose. I would have sent it before according to her orders, but waited in hopes of receiving a letter from her, that I might be able to acquaint you of her safe arrival in

France; but as I have not heard from her since, I judged it not right to delay sending you this letter and its inclosure any longer.

"I hope you have heard from her before now. I have a box of clothes belonging to her, as also a check on the bank for 25, which she desired me to send to you in case of any thing happening to her. She sent by Betsey Dinner, two gowns to her sister, before she went to France. I almost forgot to mention, that her child died about a fortnight before she left London.

"You will please to answer this by return of post, as I mean to write to her shortly.

"I am, Sir, with respect, your very humble Servant,

"ELIZABETH FLOWER."

"Please to direct to me at No. 24, Wilmot Street, Brunswick Square, London."

"For Mr. Thomas Willcocks,

"Witheridge, near Crediton, Devonshire."

Mrs. Worrall, having thus obtained corroborative testimony of the truth of the principal occurrences of the last eight years of the life of her Protegée, and also possession of the letters which her parents gave to the gentleman who visited Witheridge, and which contained the addresses of the different families in which she had been in service in the metropolis, agreed, with the full approbation and consent of the girl, to procure her a passage for America, to which country her mind was fully bent on proceeding. The Robert and Ann, Capt. Robertson, had at that time nearly completed her cargo, and was about to sail from Bristol for Philadelphia. In this vessel Mrs. W. agreed with the Captain for her passage, and furnished her with clothes and money sufficient to support her, till she could find a service in Philadelphia; and three young females of Bristol, who were going in the same ship to that city, as teachers in a Moravian establishment there, were prevailed upon to notice and protect her during her voyage;[1] at the termination of which, should they approve of her conduct, Mrs. W. with the same kindness and liberality which she had uniformly extended towards her, authorised the ladies to present her with farther pecuniary assistance.

Before the departure of Caraboo, the public curiosity to gain a sight of her was rather increased than diminished. The Earl of C—k came from Bath for the sole purpose of conversing with her. The Marquis of S—y wrote to request the same indulgence, but she was supposed to have left Bristol. She was in fact visited by persons of all descriptions—natives and foreigners, linguists, painters, physiognomists, craniologists, and gypsies; all were anxious to see and converse with this female Psalmanazar. Some pitied her, some condemned her, & others upheld her. Of her being a Christian there was now no doubt; and Mrs. W.'s first wish was to have placed her in some pious family. She was therefore preached to and prayed by; but the visits of the divines made no impression, as one of them said, on her impenetrable heart. She continued under the roof of Mr. Mortimer till her departure. During which time she shewed no signs of contrition for the part she had been acting, but appeared highly gratified and proud of the number of dupes and proselytes, who had attached themselves to her for such a length of time. It would be unjust, however, not to except Mrs. Worrall from this general charge of want of feeling and ingratitude. She certainly did not appear insensible of her great kindness and unwearied attentions to her comfort and happiness, and the day before she sailed, she left the following singular epistle, directed to Mrs. W. which is here copied verbatim:—

"friendship thou charmer of the mind thou sweet deluding ill the brightest moments mortals find and sharpest pains can

---

1. It has been asserted, that she was *smuggled* on board this vessel; the assertion is false. She was regularly entered as a passenger, not in the name of *Baker* it is true, but in that of *Burgess,* her mother's maiden name. This was done from no other motive than to prevent the visits and enquiries of strangers.

feel fate has divided all our shares of pleasure and of pain in love the friendship and the cares are mixed and join again the same ingenious author in another place says tis dangerous to let loose our love between the eternal fair for pride that busy sin spoils all that we perform."

One of the Moravian Ladies has also written word, that while the vessel was lying in Kingroad, she more than once shed tears, when she saw Knole[1] in the distance. Since she has left Bristol, a friend of Mrs. W.'s has visited London, and made enquiries into her mode of life and conduct there, of the several persons whose addresses were contained in the letters, which her parents received from her. The following are selected from several other very singular occurrences:—

The first person whom the enquirer sought for was the Rev. Mr. Pattenden, a dissenting clergyman, who lives at No. 29, Coppice-Row, Spafields. Mr. Pattenden confirmed all that the girl had told of his knowledge of her; that he took her out of the Hospital, procured her the place at Mrs. Matthews's, got her child into the Foundling-Hospital, and his daughter, who had gone to enquire after it, was informed that it was dead. She had told him, that its father was the master of a family in whose service she had lived in the country. That during a twelvemonth he had lost sight of her; that his family always took a great interest in her welfare, and whenever she was out of place or wanted help, she applied to them. They did not think there was any harm in her; but she was always so odd and eccentric, that Mr. P. said it would fill a volume, if he were to transcribe all that he knew of her. The following letter has been since received from Miss Pattenden, in answer to one written by Mrs. W.'s friend, to ascertain some dates more accurately:

"Hon. Madam,
"Agreeable to your request, I write to you what further information I can respecting Mary Willcocks; we suppose,

---

1. Knole is a very conspicuous land-mark looking up the Bristol Channel.

Madam, that she lie-in in February 1816, as to the place where, her account was contradictory; to one she said, the child was born on the road to London; to another she said, she lie-in at Westminster lying-in hospital. The child was taken into the Foundling the 6th day of July 1816, and we suppose was baptized there, and we think it lived about two months after, or a little more; we have not seen her I believe since last Christmas. The family she lived with at Islington, was a Mrs. Starling's, the corner of Norfolk Street, near the Thatched House, the lower part of Islington. The pay she said she received for the child was from Lambeth workhouse, and it is likely they can give some account of the father;[1] her story in this, as in many other matters, varied. To some she said it was by her master, a French gentleman at Exeter; to others she said it was by a young gentleman under his care; and to others, that the father was a labouring man who worked at her master's; this she said at the Foundling, and that his name was Baker. I think, Madam, you have the address of Mrs. Matthews, No. 1, Clapham-road Place, where she lived soon after we first had knowledge of her! I wish, Madam, we could give you more information; and I sincerely pray, notwithstandingall her past conduct, which displays such great wickedness, the Lord may give her grace to repent; and that in some future day we may hear of her being a bright and shining character, one that truly fears God and departs from all iniquity.

"I am, dear Madam, your very humble Servant,

"P. Pattenden."

"29, Coppice Row, Spa Fields."

"July 15th, 1817."

He next enquiry was made at the Crab-tree public-house, in Tottenham-Court Road, kept by a Mrs. Clark. She lived there

---

1. Nothing can be traced respecting her here.

six months, and staid till she was taken in labour; but she did not go to the City Lying-in Hospital, as she herself stated to Mrs. W. She took a hackney coach, when she left the Crab-tree, and went on the Bayswater road. The coachman, who drove her, was curious to find out, where she was going, and after he put her down, he watched her, but, with her usual dexterity, she eluded him; and though she called at the Crab-tree afterwards, with the child in her arms, they never could find out where she lie-in. During the six months she lived there, she conducted herself with the greatest propriety; was particularly modest in her behaviour, and one of the most cleanly, regularly, good servants they ever had. She then passed by the name of Hannah; but in a Bible, which she used to read on a Sunday, the name of MARY BAKER was written. She told them, her husband was dead, but they thought she never had been married. They were very partial to her. She scarcely ever went out; but told such odd unaccountable stories, that she became proverbial amongst them for the marvellous; they were stories, however, which never did harm to any body, but seemed to arise from the love of telling something extraordinary.

Mr. Cole and the family, mentioned in one of her letters as living at No. 24, Wilmot-Street, also spoke well of her character, but nothing particular transpired from them, except that she left Wilmot-Street on account of being with child.

From Mrs. Field and Mrs. Ferret, who were living at No. 32, Thornaugh-Street, according to the direction in the letter, but who had removed to No. 18, Cumberland-Street, New-Road, Mrs. W.'s friend found, that the girl had lived with them six months, had conducted herself to their satisfaction, and was a very pleasing good servant.

Mrs. Matthews was the next person called upon.—Mrs. W.'s friend describes this lady as a most worthy excellent woman. She was pleased to see her, and had frequently thought of writing to Mrs. W. since she had heard of CARABOO in the newspapers. She confirmed the account which Caraboo and Mr. Pattenden had given of her having lived three years in

her service; that she had the illness in her house, which she
described; that her conduct was always correct in every respect,
except that she told terrible stories, yet after all they were such
as did no injury to others, or good to herself. Her behaviour was
always so strange and eccentric, and her ways so mysterious,
that Mrs. M. said, that no one who did not know the girl would
believe them, were she to relate what occurred. That she ran
away from her suddenly, on finding Mr. Pattenden was coming
to talk with her, for having played some unaccountable prank, or
told some unaccountable story. Notwithstanding the eccentricity
of her conduct, Mrs. M. was very partial to her, and every one,
who came to her house and saw her, took an interest in her; that
she was a very capable, good servant, and seldom went out;
that she would sometimes say, she would not eat for several
days together, to shew how long she could live without food;
that she had left her service about four years, but in the course
of that period, had called several times upon her. Once she
called to say, that a gentleman from the Foundling, would wait
on Mrs. M. for her character, and if she spoke well of her, her
child would be admitted there. The gentleman came, and the
child was taken in. The last time she saw her was in November
1816; she said, she was in place at Islington, that her child was
dead, and she was dressed in mourning. She then told Mrs.
M. that the child's father was a bricklayer. It was through Mr.
Pattenden, that Mrs. M. first took her. Mr. P. had gone to St.
Giles's Workhouse, to pray with a sick young woman, he saw
Mary, and found she was to be dismissed the next day; that she
was friendless, and thought it was a pity she should be thrown
on the wide world, and Mrs. M. being in want of a servant, took
her on the emergency. Mrs. M.'s daughter, who taught her to
write, is no more. Neither Mrs. Matthews nor Mr. Pattenden
thought she had ever been abroad, though they considered
it not impossible, as they lost sight of her at intervals, for a
considerable time.

In consequence of the information in Miss Pattenden's letter,
enquiries were made at Mr. Starling's, the corner of Norfolk-
Street, near the Thatched-House, Islington, where she went

to live in July 1816, and continued until November, when she was dismissed, for setting two beds on fire in the course of one week!![1] The motive was, that a fellow-servant, whom she did not like, might be suspected and sent away. Though Mrs. Starling did not think she meant to let the fire proceed to such an height, that she could not herself extinguish it, yet having played her trick, she could never sleep in peace while she was under her roof. That she was the best servant she ever had in her house, but so odd and eccentric, that she frequently thought she must be out of her mind. She was very fond of her children, but told them such strange stories about gypsies and herself, that she frightened them out of their wits. She once came into the parlour, and had dressed herself up so like a gypsey, that the children did not know her. She told them she had been in the East-Indies and America; that she was in Philadelphia; was brought to bed by the side of a river; that a lady and gentleman going by in a carriage took her up, and had her taken care of. Mrs. Starling could not recollect a quarter of her vagaries. She went to Mrs. Starling's just as her child died; made her mourning there, and so quick, that they were surprised when she put it on. They did not know, who the father of the child was. She said, she had been married by a Catholic priest to a Frenchman, who had left her, and the child had died at her mother's. She used to go somewhere to receive money, as she said, once a month, but they could never discover where. In short, the part she played with them was incredible; yet they liked her, and had it not been for the affair of the fire, would have kept her. When Mr. and Mrs. Starling read the story of Caraboo in the papers, they recognised the servant that had lived with them, and thought of writing to Mrs. Worrall about her, but feared, if she discovered that they had interfered, she

---

1. Undoubtedly the greatest blot upon her character! But as the present Narrative may be depended upon as *a statement of every materiel fact,* which has been deemed worth recording relative to this singular creature, it would have been wrong to suppress such an occurrence.

would have returned to London, and waylaid Mr. Starling in his walks home, through the fields to Islington.

The information gained at the Magdalen Hospital was as follows:

"ANNE BURGESS—admitted into the Magdalen-Hospital February 14th, 1813, and discharged at her own request July 22nd, 1813,

"Stated, she was born November 11th, 1792; that her parents were dead; that her father died when she was a month old; that he was a shoemaker, at Witheridge, in Devonshire; that her mother had been dead four years and a half; that her mother on her death-bed recommended her daughter (A.B.) To the protection of the Rev. Mr. Luxham, Minister of Reckingford, near Witheridge; that he took her into his service, in which she was seduced by a gentleman who visited the family, who brought her to London, lived with her a month, when he deserted her, and she went on the town, and led a loose life; said she had been in an hospital two years before.

"After being in the house, acknowledged the preceding account of herself was untrue, except that her father died in her infancy; her name not *Burgess;* no such person as Rev. Mr. Luxham; had a female friend at Exeter; did not know of her misconduct; said to the women, she had assumed the name of Willcocks and Baker, and that she had lived (in 1811) in service in the Clapham-Road, and in Edgeware-Road.

"During the short time she was in the Magdalen Hospital, her conduct was very eccentric; she did not betray any propensity to vice, but was unsettled from the time of her admission, till she left the house.[1] Much pains being

---

1. The following memorandum was made by one of the officers, during her continuance in the house, relative to her conduct: *"Anne Burgess* conducts herself with great propriety, and seems *repentant almost to despondence."*

taken to persuade her to disclose who her friends were, she became more restless than before; said, if it was discovered who she was, she would hang herself. On the 8th and 15th of July, she asked for her discharge; but, with much solicitation, was prevailed on to stay until the 29th of the same month, when no further entreaty had any weight; said then, she was not a fallen woman, and that she had been married, but would disclose nothing further. On the day after her discharge, she called at the house, not in the tattered clothes in which she left the house on the preceding day, but in others of a better quality, and said, she had a box of clothes at a friend's. Heard no more of her till October 15th, 1814, when she called at the Magdalen Hospital, very decent in her dress, general appearance and manners; said, that she had walked to Exeter since she left the Magdalen, and at Exeter found her former mistress, Mrs. Partridge (whose town-house is in Bloomsbury-Square); was going with her to France in the capacity of a cook; had told Mrs. P. she had been in the Magdalen Hospital, and that Mrs. P. said, I know the Magdalen very well, and I hope you will never forget the good advice you received there."

Upon computing the time that she lived with Mrs. Matthews, her service with Mrs. Clark at the Crab-tree, her continuance in the Magdalen, and in other places, it appears that the last eight years of her life are nearly accounted for; and her assertion, that she had been in the East or in America, must have been one of those unaccountable fictions, in which she so strangely indulged. To whom she was married, or who was the father of her child, are also some of those events in her life, which have hitherto baffled every attempt to ascertain the truth.

The foregoing Narrative lays claim to no other attention from the public, than the *Detail of Facts* which it contains of the singular adventures and unparalleled success in deception, which this Young Female practised, undiscovered, for the space of nearly ten weeks. That an illiterate girl, unaided by education, in her usual manners and common appearance by no means elegant or striking, and with no apparent object, but an ambition to excel in deceit, should have so conducted herself both in the language she made use of, and in her general demeanor, as to have induced hundreds to believe, that she was no less a personage than an unfortunate, unprotected, and wandering Princess from a distant Eastern Island, cast upon the shores of Britain by cruel and relentless Pirates;—that she should have sustained this character, with a countenance never changed by the abject flattery, or the most abusive invective, constantly surrounded by persons of superior talent and education, as well as by those in her own rank of life, who were always on the watch to mark any inconsistency, or to catch at any occurrence that could lead to detection;—and that on no occasion was she found to lose sight of the part she was acting, or once to betray herself;—is an instance of consummate art and duplicity exceeding any occurrence in the annals of modern imposture,[1] The fasting woman of Tetbury, Johanna Southcote, the famous cheats and disguises of Bampfield More Carew himself do not exhibit cunning, talent, and perseverance half so extraordinary. The weapons of imposition, which she handled with so much dexterity, were, it is true, furnished her by her admiring spectators; for although Caraboo could not speak a word of English, Mary Willcocks could, and she could hear it and profit by it too. The principal words she used, which smattered of Malay, Arabic,

---

1. It is omitted to be stated in the page in which her Bath visit is recorded, that so fully persuaded was one gentleman of the reality of the fiction, and so highly had she worked upon his feelings, that he declared in her presence, he would willingly subscribe 500. to send her home to Javasu, or to whatever island it should be discovered, that she belonged. A collection was once indeed set on foot before her, and bank-notes were strewed on the table; but with her usual *non chalance,* she picked them up as so many pieces of blank paper—for what were black-letter tens and twenties, with the words BANK OF ENGLAND staring her in the face, to her, who could neither read or write the English language!

and other Eastern languages, some she learned no doubt from the foreigner with whom she co-habited, and others from the gypsies with whom, it is not improbable, she resided a longer time than she thought it prudent to disclose. The characters which she wrote, she copied from her recollection, by a glance she caught of different Eastern languages exhibited to her in books, and written before her at Knole. Her acquaintance with Indian manners, habits, &c. she obtained from the different persons who visited her, and who had been in India, and were all eager to display their knowledge to the surrounding auditory; and which the listening and cunning Caraboo eagerly imbibed, as readily imitated, and never failed to turn to account.

That the talents of such a girl should have been hitherto directed to no better purpose, every one must lament. Her object in visiting America could never be correctly developed. That she had some wild and desperate enterprise in view, appeared from her telling one of her enquirers, that she predicted she should return to England in her carriage and four horses. Poor, visionary, deluded girl!!

But what shall be said of all the learned travellers, the philosophers, to cognoscenti, the blue stocking ladies, and the numerous dupes of various denominations, who were so completely juggled and out-witted?—They must console themselves with the doctrines of Hudibras,

> *"That the pleasure is as great*
> *"In being cheated, as to cheat."*
>
> —*Butler*

In regard to Mrs. Worrall, should any reflection be thrown upon her character, for the part which she had acted, she has no doubt ample consolation in the benevolent feelings which animated her bosom, and induced her, through every stage of the imposition, to be active and zealous in well-doing.

A Vocabulary of Words, with Their Meanings, Made Use of by Caraboo

Allah Tallah: *God*
Samen: *Heaven*
Tarsa: *Earth*
Mordains: *the Malay*
Buis, or Bugos: *any Wild People*
Manjintoo: *Gentlemen*
Lazor: *Ladies*
Makrittoo: *Servant Men*
Somens: *Servant Women*
Justo or Justu: *Doctor*
Kala: *Time*
Alkader: *Lot, Destiny*
Mono: *Morning*
Anna: *Night*
Vellee: *Bed*
Apa: *Fire*
Ana: *Water*
Savee: *Rain*
Meller: *Yes*
Beck: *Good*
No bo: *No good*
Dosi: *Dinner*
Sacco: *Supper*
Ake Brasidoo: *Come to Breakfast*
Ake Dosi: *Come to Dinner*
Ake Sacco: *Come to Supper*

Zee: *Tea*
Suso: *Sugar*
Passa: *Flour*
Mo: *Milk*
Bras: *Rice*
Pakey: *Child*
Vatan: *Gown*
Mozum: *Fish*
Tamah: *Fowl*
Rampue or Rambu: *a Pigeon*
Nee: *Egg*
Archee: *Potato*
Oree: *Onions*
Savoo: *a Knife*
Foso: *a Fork*
Oser: *Salt*
Makey: *Pepper*
Arra: *an Eclipse*
Sanatoo: *the Sun*
Toree: *a Stone*
Bardoo: *Dead*
Smache: *Cayenne*
Botee: *an Arrow*
Doteau: *Gold Dust*
Sirrea: *Mother of Pearl*
Nontee: *an Orange*
Botin: *the Head*
Nater: *the Arm*
Nease: *the Foot*
Tenzenee: *a Sail*
Tuzar: *a Ship*
Bosve: *a Boat*
Toose: *to swim*
Paza: *Peacock's Feathers*
Puloponnaung: *a Word in common use in Malay, literally the Betel Nut Island in the Straits of Malacca*

Khalifaton, Kader, Zimam, Ziban: *Words to which she affixed no determinate meaning*

Prabha: *Head*

Indue: *her Father's Country*

Induis: *her Mother's Country*

Inju Jagoos: *Do not be afraid.*

The Following Were the Few Gypsey Words Which She Used

Mosha: *a Man*

Raglish: *a Woman*

Gosha: *a Landlady*

Tanee: *a Halfpenny*

Win: *a Penny*

Tanner: *a Sixpence*

Bob: *a Shilling*

Junk: *two Shillings*

Bub: *five Shillings.*

Characters Made Use of by Caraboo, and Her Autograph of Mary Baker

The lettered reader will perceive a few perfectly-formed and conjoined Arabic characters; it need not to be added, that she copied them from those which some Oriental Scholar wrote before her.

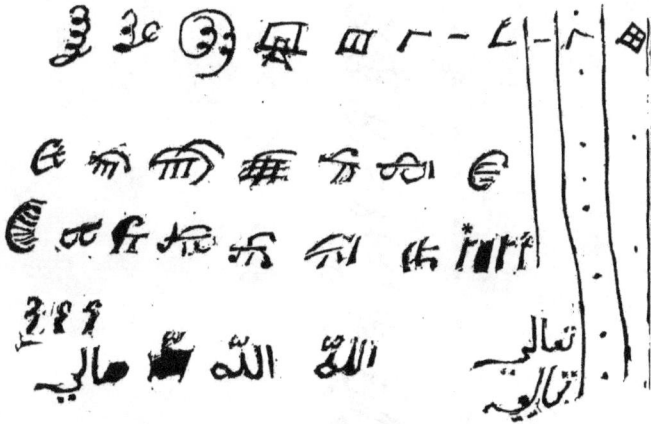

* Allah-Tallah ("word" at end of third line)

Numerical Characters, with Their Significations, Made Use of by Caraboo

1		Eze
2		Duce
3		Trua
4		Tan
5		Zennee
6		Sendee
7		Tam
8		Nunta
9		Berteen
10		Tashman
11		Limmenee
12		Judgbennee
13		Artinne
14		Ferney
15		Fissmen
		Infuse red paint,

Chart, of Her Voyage to Europe, Drawn by Caraboo

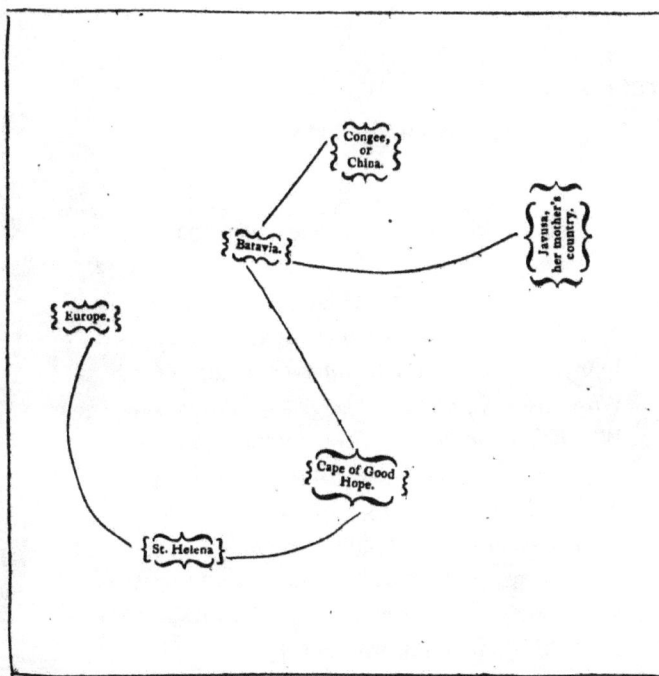

Congee, or China.

Javuse, her mother's country.

Batavia.

Europe.

Cape of Good Hope.

St. Helena

Poems and Articles

The following JEU D'ESPRITS *appeared in the different* BRISTOL *and* BATH NEWSPAPERS, *during the period which this imposture formed a topic of public conversation.*

Caraboo
(From the Bath Herald)

> *Oh! aid me, ye spirits of wonder! who soar*
> *In realms of Romance where none ventur'd before;*
> *Ye Fairies! who govern the fancies of men,*
> *And sit on the point of Monk Lewis's pen;*
> *Ye mysterious Elves! who for ever remain*
> *With Lusus Naturæs and Ghosts of Cock-lane;*
> *Who ride upon broom-sticks, intent to deceive*
> *All those who appear pre-disposed to believe,*
> *And softly repeat from your home in the spheres*
> *Incredible stories to credulous ears;*
> *With every thing marvellous, every thing new,*
> *We'll trace a description of Miss CARABOO.*
> *JOHANNA's disciples, who piously came*
> *To present babies' caps to their elderly dame,*
> *Though all hope of their virgin's accouchement is o'er,*
> *They shall meet with the smile of derision no more;*
> *Their wonders were weak, their credulity small—*
> *Caraboo was engendered by nothing at all!*

And where did she come from? and who can she be?
Did she fall from the sky? did she rise from the sea?
A seraph of day, or a shadow of night?
Did she spring upon earth in a stream of gas-light?
Did she ride on the back of a fish, or sea-dog?
A spirit of health, or a devil incog.?
Was she wafted by winds over mountains and stream?
Was she borne to our isle by the impulse of steam?
Was she found in complete "fascination" elate?
Or discovered at first in a chrysalis state?
Did some philosophic analysis draw
Her competent degrees from some hot-water spa?
Did some chemical process occasion her birth?
Did galvanic experiments bring her on earth?
Is she new? is she old? is she false? is she true?
Come read me the riddle of Miss Caraboo.
Astronomers sage may exhibit her soon
As daughter-in-law to the man in the moon;
Or declare that her visit accounts for the rain,
Which happened last year, and may happen again;
That dark spots appear in the course she has run,
Coeval perhaps with the spots in the sun;
That she may be connected with corsairs; all these,
And as many more possible things as you please.
In what hand does she write?—in what tongue does she
                                          speak?

Is it Arabic, Persic, Egyptian, or Greek?
She must be a blue-stocking lady indeed,
To write an epistle which no man can read;
Though we have some publishing scribes I could name,
Whose letters will meet with a fate much the same.
She then wore no ear-rings, tho' still may be seen
The holes in her ears, where her ear-rings have been;
Leather shoes on her feet; a black shawl round her hair;
And of black worsted stockings an elegant pair;
Her gown was black-stuff, and my readers may guess,

If her story contains as much stuff as her dress.
Of the fam'd Indian Jugglers we all must have heard,
Who to gain a subsistence would swallow a sword;
But men (without proof) who believe tales like these,
Will undoubtedly swallow whatever you please.
I have heard, those who thought, that she wished to
                                                    deceive,
After seeing her person have learned to believe;
Even those, who have doubted the truth of her case,
Have forgotten their doubts when they look'd in her face.
I have never see her; but if when I see,
The truth of her tale is apparent to me,
I will cancel these lines, and most gladly rehearse
Her swimming and fencing in beautiful verse;
In the graces and charms of my muse to adorn her,
Shall be the employment of
Q IN THE CORNER
Bath, June 10, 1817.

Ode to Miss Molly Baker, alias Princess Caraboo
(From the Bristol Mercury)

O Molly, what a wag thou art—
So effectually to play the part
Of wandering, friendless Caraboo,
Bespeaks a talent few could boast
Ev'n from a juggling India's coast—
But prythee, tell me—can it ALL be true?
If thou, when heather Greek inditing
Didst rival RAPIER in his writing—
(So versatile thy nature,
And sweetly plastic every limb),
Like ROLAND fence, like Dolphin swim—

Thou art indeed an interesting creature.
Wert thou with ALL the men so shy,
As ev'n thy beauteous hand deny
In common salutation?
Was there no tender téte-a-téte,
Thy admirers thus to fascinate,
Who puff'd thy beauty through the nation?
Thy sloe-black eyes, and teeth so white,
(By Nature form'd to charm or bite)
With lady-airs in plenty—
Like opiates all the senses lull'd,
Of reason and of reason gulled,
Th' all-knowing Cognoscenti.
When to the house-top prone to stray,
And would'st to ALLA-TALLAH pray,
Had'st thou no HIGH PRIEST near thee?
I mean not that imperious sun
Of reckless Juggernaut, but ONE
Well pleas'd to assist and hear thee?
But where did'st learn (for Heav'n's sake),
To swim and dive like duck or drake,
When water-dogs pursue?
And when for pure ablution quipp'd,
Lurk'd there (as when Godiva stripp'd)
No Peeping Tom—or wanton Makratoo?
Plague on that meddling tell-tale NEALE,
Eager thy hist'ry to reveal,
And mar the pleasing fable:—
Too sudden came the denouement,
Which proves thou art from down-along,
Where dumplings grace each table.
"Drat her pug nose, and treacherous eyes,
"Deceitful wretch!" the Doctor cries,
(No more inclin'd to flattery;)
"When next I meet her (spite of groans)
"I'll rive her muscles, split her bones

"With my Galvanic Battery."
But heed him not—for ('on my soul)
Whether at Bristol, Bath, or Knole,
I admir'd thy Caraboo.
Such self-possession at command,
The bye-play great—th' illusion grand:
In truth—'twas every thing but TRUE.
Then Molly, take a friend's advice,
(To make thy fortune in a trice)
All wand'ring gypsey tricks resign—
Fly to thy proper forte—the STAGE:
Where thou in this half-mimic age,
Princess of Actors, would'st unrivall'd shine!!!
X.
Bristol, June 21st, 1817.

Young Caraboo!—a Parody
(From the Bristol Mirror)

[See "YOUNG LOCHINVAR," in "MARMION."]
O young Caraboo is come out of the West,
In frenchified tatters the damsel is drest;
But, save one pair of worsted, she stockings had none,
She walk'd half unshod, and she walk'd all alone;
But how to bamboozle the doxy well knew—
There never was gipsey like young Caraboo.
She staid not for brake, and she stopp'd not for stone,
She swam in the Avon where ford there was none;
But when she alighted at Worralby gate,
The Dame and the Doctor received her in state;
No longer a gipsey, the club of Bas-bleu
To a Princess converted the young Caraboo.
So boldly she enter'd the Worralby Hall,

Amidst linguists, skull-feelers, blue stockings, and all;
Then spoke the sage doctor, profoundly absurd,
(But sly Caraboo utter'd never a word)
"Art thou sprung from the Moon, or from far Javasu,
Or a Mermaid just landed, thou bright Caraboo!"
To these questions sagacious she answer denied—
'Tho' hard was the struggle her laughter to hide—
"But, since they decree me these titles do fine,
I'll be silent, eat curry, and touch not their wine;
With this imposition I've done nothing to do;
These are fools ready made"—thought the young Caraboo.
She looked at a pigeon, the dame caught it up;
Caraboo had a mind on the pigeon to sup.
She look'd down to titter, she look'd up to sigh,
With the bird in her hand, and the spit in her eye,
She dress'd it, she ate it, she call'd it Rampoo—
"This proves," swore the Doctor, "she's Queen Caraboo."
When she fenc'd with the Doctor, so queer her grimace,
Sure never a hall such a galliard did grace;
But her Host seem'd to fret (tho' the Doctor did fume,
Should any to question her titles presume,)
And 'twas currently whisper'd, the best they could do,
Was to send up to London young Queen Caraboo.
The hint was enough; as it dropp'd on her ear
It ruin'd her hopes. It awaken'd her fear;
So light to the Quay the fair damsel she ran,
"Oh take me, dear Captain, away if you can!"
She's aboard! She is gone! "Farewell Doctor Rampoo;
They'll have swift ships that follow," said young Caraboo.
There was bustling 'mong dames of the Worralby clan;
The Blue-stocking Junto they rode and they ran;
There was racing and chasing from Bath to the Sea,
But the lost Queen of Javasu ne'er more did they see.
What a hoax on the Doctor, and club of Bas-bleu!
Have ye e'er heard of gipsey like young Caraboo?

Sporting Intelligence Extra!
(From the Bristol Mirror)

Caraboo is entered to run for the Knole plate! She is thought
by all who have seen her to be the cleverest *mare* in this part of
the country, being very perfect in all her paces, an easy pleasant
goer, and of great speed. She is well bred, shews a good deal of
both blood and bone, and has an admirable forehand. She is
5 feet 2, and rising 26. Caraboo's pedigree is warranted to be
true *Circassian;* got by the *Chinese Corsair,* JESSUE MANDUE,
out of a Devonshire Gipsey; own sister to FORTUNE TELLER.
She has been long favorite with the turf; and has been lately
in famous training (about a mile from Almondsbury) at the
mews of LEUMAS LLARROW, Eritiqse, many years well known
as a keen Glocestershire *Sportsman,* and an excellent *Judge*—
of horse-flesh! Her feeder assures every body, that her mode
of dieting seems to be *Hindoo-stanie,* as she lives principally
on vegetables, and has no objection to *curry*-combing! She is
rather dainty; prefers going to the pond instead of drinking
out of the bucket; and has once or twice taken a *swim,* to the
astonishment of the stable-boys. This is chiefly after galloping
about in the SUN, which she seems almost to adore—this the
Cognoscenti suppose is caused by *his* being the patron of Hay-
makers; but upon this point, there is a difference of opinion.
Though quite free from vice, she kicks with great dexterity; but
it is all an idle report that she gives out the near leg behind to a
lady, and the off one before to a gentleman! There is however a
peculiarity about her, which is, that she winces if the stable-boy
only touches her housings. The master of the mews one day
happening only just to pat her neck, she began to neigh like a
filly, so tremendously that the like was never before heard in
that quarter. How Caraboo ever came to submit to be *hugged*
in the *mane,* and *fired,* is most surprising; though it is indeed
stated, that the latter was not performed after the English
method, or after any European fashion whatsoever. We learn
too, that "she is shod with leather;" from which circumstance
it seems certain, that there are people who know the length

of her foot! It is acknowledged, that she is fond of playing at hide and seek, and is very apt to *bolt*.

She is so very hard mouthed, that the vetrinarians of Oxford, Cambridge, and the India House, have been unable to find a *bit* that will suit her; although an exact fac-simile of her *blarney* has been sent to them, upon a species of papyrus. Her jabber-nowl, notwithstanding "her mouth is rather large," is so beautiful and prepossessing, that a *bird's-eye view* of it has been taken by an eminent Artist, and will no doubt form a very interesting study for the lovers of the *Arabesque.*

The followers of Doctors GALL and SPURZHEIM will learn with great pleasure, that Caraboo has been *Craniologized* by several Ladies of distinction, and that she exhibits numbers 1, 2, 9, 12, and 32, in great perfection. Indeed it is the finest specimen of number 12 ever seen since the days of GEORGE PSALMANAZAR—the late JOHANNA SOUTHCOTT, and the Tetbury Fasting Woman not excepted.

When she starts for the Knole plate, her rider will be one JUSTEE, a famous Jockey from Bath. He will run her against *Cho, Abacus, Suonpuon, Iota, Pi, Epsilon,* and other noted horses, whose names may be seen at the Kingston Pump-Room.

This match has excited uncommon bustle amongst the *Greeks, Malayans, Chinese, Shanscritians, Arabians, Persians, Sumatrans,*—and ALLAH TALLAH only knows how many *Ans* besides.

Some disputes however have arisen respecting the long odds, for which no authority can be found either in the *Polyglot, Fry's Pantographia, Hager's Elementaria,* or WILKINSON'S *Humbugania!*—so that it is thought this TAIL *of Mystery* will be referred to the *Town-clerk* and the *Macratoos* (gentlemen of the long robe) at the ensuing Quarter Sessions for the city and county of *Javasu!!!*

Craniological Description of Caraboo
(From the Bristol Mirror)

Although many of our Readers think the system of Dr. SPURZHEIM altogether fanciful, yet others continue of a differ-

ent opinion. At all events, it may be curious to observe how far
the organization of this girl's Head answers to these notions.
We shall therefore record it,—not in mere jest, but as a matter
of information.

Judging by this index, we should say, that she was consti-
tutionally cold, and indifferent to physical love—or, to speak
more intelligibly, not amorous. She was boundless AMBITION;
indeed this organ is so strongly marked, that to be thought a
PRINCESS would be to her the *summum bonum*. She has great
ATTACHMENT, or capability of firm friendship; no quarrelsome-
ness, or wish to injure any one—which is, in the idiom of the
science, no COMBATIVENESS, or DESTRUCTIVENESS. Not the
least COVETIVENESS; that is, she is perfectly indifferent to the
acquirement or keeping of money or property. She has com-
paratively very little SECRETIVENESS: this organ is the one by
which, the GALL-ites say, the possesser keeps his own secret,—
wraps himself up in impenetrable mystery,—keeping all real
knowledge of himself and his intentions carefully concealed in
his own heart, under a specious exterior. Now, how is it possible,
that this organ, which it might be supposed CARABOO would
have in the greatest perfection, should be defective, or how far
her general conduct actually squares with it in point of fact, we
leave to others to determine, contenting ourselves with recording the fact. The paradox will appear the wider when we state
that she has CIRCUMSPECTION or CAUTION in a *monstrous*
degree. Her WARINESS is fully equalled by her VANITY. Her
organization in this respect, if it could speak, would say plainly,
"I, I, I, it is I, who can nose-lead you, and make fools of ye all!
I am this CARABOO, about whom you have made such a *fuss!*
It is I who have had one Lady offering upon her knees '*a bowl
of cream for my Royal Highness!*'—it is I who have had another
bowing in vacant amazement at the grandeur and sublimity
of MY IMPERIAL MAJESTY!"

She has no BENEVOLENCE, but a great deal of VENERATION.
The latter would induce her to behave kindly towards her Parents; and the facts here bear the system out, for she has, from

time to time sent them money, and written affectionate letters to them. As to her VENERATION in a religious point of view, it is a feeling of the heart which can only be known to herself.

It is doubtful; whether she has IMAGINATION or IDEALITY—in other words, we cannot judge whether she could write a Novel or a Farce—although we venture to say that she herself forms an excellent SUBJECT for one.

She has INDIVIDUALITY—that is she remembers persons and things, and stores them up to be used as occasion requires. She is not wanting in FORM or COLOUR; and has IMITATION, in the greatest perfection.—She would soon rival Mr. THELWALL, or Mr. MATTHEWS in *fac-similes* of every body whom she might choose to mimic.

In a word, if there be any truth in *Craniology,* she would, to the extent of her physical powers, make an admirable Actress;[1] but she would have nothing *original:* she would borrow here and there; but she would never strike out any thing absolutely new. She has not much COMPARISON: so that probably her judgment of what is excellent and what is otherwise would not be correct. Hence she would be as apt to copy faults as perfections; but the picture would be an exact copy—her *imitation* would be *the thing itself.*

She has SPACE exceedingly developed—in other words, she must be of a roving disposition, and prefer liberty, and "the whole world before her, where to chuse," to good cheer and a collar, even although it were of gold—that is, she is fitted for a Gypsey—to which she will return, if there be faith in SPURZHEIM!—for we strongly suspect, that if the whole truth were known, she has been *three years* instead of three days amongst this ancient society of Vagabonds.

To sum up all, her *knowing faculties* infinitely outweigh her *animal propensities;*—and if there should be any attempt to

---

1. After the discovery, she more than once expressed a wish, that the tale might be dramatized; and nothing, she said, would have given her greater pleasure, than to have acted the part of CARABOO!!

reclaim this stray sheep, her Guardian must take this for his guide—*if there be any truth in Craniology!*

FINIS.

www.ingramcontent.com/pod-product-compliance
Lightning Source LLC
Chambersburg PA
CBHW031605040426
42452CB00006B/414